PRAISE FOR

Dialogues with Yeshua and Mary Magdalene

"As a teacher of Christ consciousness for 40 years, I rarely have chosen to write a review of a book. *Dialogues with Yeshua and Mary Magdalene* is one such book. The questions addressed in this book are ones most of us would love to ask if we knew the reply would be one we could count on. Mercedes has an incredible way of approaching sensitive topics, such as the errors made within the church, sexuality, dimensionality, and the seeming complexities of love. This material speaks to the heart and soul."

**—Michael Mirdad, Unity of Sedona Spiritual Leader
and author of *The Book of Love and Forgiveness***

"An empowering self-mastery guide to the healing of the Divine Feminine and the Divine Masculine within your own body, heart, and mind. Yeshua and Mary Magdalene beckon."

—Claire Heartsong, author of *Anna, Grandmother of Jesus*

"A gorgeous communication, at once profound and so accessible and relatable. Yeshua and Tom's 'man to man' dialogues are, for me as a man, immensely appealing and nurturing. Hearing Yeshua tell me that I AM God struck a chord of almost indescribable resonance in my whole being: heart, soul, mind, and body. Mercedes's channeling of these multidimensional divine personalities shines with authority and grace."

**—Saniel Bonder, founder, Waking Down® and
author of *Healing the Spirit/Matter Split***

"An extension of Yeshua and Mary Magdalene's mystery school teachings of the past, this book offers profound understanding and teachings. If you're ready for the next giant leap in your spiritual evolution, the wisdom presented in this book will undoubtedly assist you to get there!"

—Catherine Ann Clemett, author of *Are You a Magdalene?*

"A joy to read . . . full of deep insights establishing the real place of Mary Magdalene as Yeshua's spiritual partner. This book explores the nature of love in an inspirational way that many readers will find very moving."

—Stuart Wilson, co-author of *Power of the Magdalene and The Essenes*

"Expanded insights and higher perspectives, inviting the reader into their heart. I highly recommend this book."

—Linda Mary Robinson, author of *Being True to Yourself*

"As a retired Presbyterian minister, I have wrestled with some of the questions Tom raises and found much wisdom in these conversations. One of my favorite exchanges is when Tom says, 'I want to be like you, all put together,' and Yeshua replies, 'Your work is not to become me but to become you . . . To let God work through you.' May Yeshua's wise advice resonate for us all."

—Rev. Trey Hammond, co-author of
Exposure and Risk: The Great Coming Church

Dialogues with
YESHUA and
MARY MAGDALENE

The Journey to Love

Mercedes Kirkel

INTO THE HEART
Creations

RIO RANCHO, NEW MEXICO

Published by

INTO THE HEART CREATIONS

Rio Rancho, New Mexico

www.intotheheart.org

Copyright © 2021 by Mercedes Kirkel

First edition

Printed in the United States of America

Publisher's Cataloging-in-Publication Data

Names:	Kirkel, Mercedes.
Title:	Dialogues with Yeshua and Mary Magdalene : The Journey to Love / Mercedes Kirkel.
Description:	First edition. | Rio Rancho, New Mexico : Into the Heart Creations, [2021]
Identifiers:	ISBN: 978-0-9840029-4-8 (paperback) | 978-0-9840029-7-9 (ePub) | LCCN: 2021903020
Subjects:	LCSH: Channeling (Spiritualism) | Spirit writings. | Jesus Christ--New Age movement interpretations. | Mary Magdalene, Saint (Spirit) | Femininity of God. |Feminist theology. | Bible--New Age movement interpretations. | Catholic Church--New Age movement interpretations. | Spirituality. | Spiritual life. | Mind and body. | LCGFT: Spirit writings. | BISAC: BODY, MIND & SPIRIT / Channeling & Mediumship. | BODY, MIND & SPIRIT / Goddess Worship. | BODY, MIND & SPIRIT / Ancient Mysteries & Controversial.
Classification:	LCC: BF1290 .K57 2021 | DDC: 133.93--dc23

3 5 7 9 10 8 6 4 2

Book design by Michelle M. White

To Yeshua and Mary Magdalene,
with immense gratitude for your unceasing blessings and help.

Only from the heart can you touch the sky.

—Rumi

Contents

Dialogues with
YESHUA *and*
MARY MAGDALENE

Introduction

I communicate with higher beings, such as Mary Magdalene[1] and Yeshua (Jesus).[2] I call what I do "channeling." I believe I've been channeling for lifetimes. I don't know how I do it; it's just natural for me.

I met Tom, a former priest, when he came to me for a channeled session with Yeshua and Mary Magdalene. Tom's wife, Ann, had been a follower of mine for years, and she had urged him to have a session with me, hoping it would resolve the unanswered questions he wrestled with relative to the Bible, the Church, and New Age spirituality.

When we began his session, neither Tom nor I realized what was to come—that this would be the first in a series of meetings with Yeshua and Mary that would span three years. And we definitely didn't fathom where these interactions would eventually lead.

While Ann is mentioned many times in these encounters, she wasn't present for any of the sessions. It was just Tom, me, Yeshua, and sometimes Mary Magdalene. My role as the one who was channeling was to set myself aside, so the higher beings could come through in a pure form. Accordingly, I wasn't a participant in the dialogues, but Tom, Yeshua, and Mary were nonetheless aware of my presence and occasionally referred to me.

Right from the beginning, these exchanges felt important to me. I had total trust in Yeshua and Mary, not only relative to the profound guidance they were bringing forth but also in their steering of the whole process. It was remarkable to watch it unfold. I offer this inspiring story just as it happened, a testament to the consummate skill and immense love of Yeshua and Mary Magdalene as they helped a spiritual brother reach a new level of being.

ONE

Tom

*T*his book came as a complete surprise to me. It certainly wasn't in my conscious plan for my life!

One day while I was listening to a channeling of Yeshua (Jesus)[3] and Mary Magdalene[4] by Mercedes Kirkel, I experienced a strong desire to speak to them myself. During my many years as a priest and afterward, I'd accumulated a plethora of questions, many of which I was afraid to ask aloud. Some seemed to have been answered to others' satisfaction but not to mine. I still wanted to understand so many things.

Eventually, I decided to have a channeled session with Mercedes, with the hope that Yeshua and Mary Magdalene would finally set my mind at peace. I immediately began pouring out my questions, as if I would never get another chance. Once I stopped and gave Yeshua an opportunity to speak, he startled me by asking if I would ask these same questions in a public forum. I was taken aback, but he said it would help others, so I agreed to do so.

Initially, I felt awkward speaking with Yeshua. Hearing a woman's voice communicate for him was confusing. *Was this really Yeshua I was speaking to?* And I'd always called him "Jesus." Yet, over the course of our conversations, I became comfortable with all this.

During these sessions, Yeshua and Mary Magdalene spoke to me with such tenderness, warmth, patience, and caring. I felt affirmed and loved. Never was I told that my questions were inappropriate. Yeshua's humor often took me by surprise, but it also carried me into deeper levels of freedom and joy.

Sometimes during our conversations, there were long pauses as I engaged a process Yeshua was leading me into. He always gave me the time I needed. He often spoke very slowly, which I sensed was to help me take in what he had to say.

That Yeshua asked me to share my questions publicly wasn't the only thing that amazed me. All of Yeshua's responses were revelatory. Some were eye opening, others almost shocking. But the biggest surprise was when he began asking *me* questions!

These dialogues have changed my life. They've changed the way I see things and how I feel. They've given me a completely different orientation to living my life. Many say that Yeshua came to heal and change lives two thousand years ago, but what's documented in this book is a testament to how Yeshua and Mary Magdalene are still healing and changing lives today, in the twenty-first century—certainly for me, and I trust for others too.

TWO

The Journey Begins

Mary Magdalene: Hello, beloved. This is Mary Magdalene.

Yeshua: Greetings. This is Yeshua.

Mary Magdalene: We're both very happy to join with you today and to help you in whatever way we're able. Thank you for calling upon us. How may we assist you?

Tom: I have issues that I haven't been able to resolve, which seem to be blocking me in moving forward with my spiritual goals and intentions.

I was brought up in a devout Catholic family and served as a priest for twenty years. Eventually, I left the priesthood and got married to a beautiful woman. I can't imagine how much she loves me and why she even does. She's so sensitive—sensitive to beauty and to pain. She weeps among flowers or when people are suffering. I wish I could be so sensitive. She's so good to me. If I say something negative, she says, "Can you rephrase that to be more positive?"

Leaving the priesthood—and deciding whether to leave the Church altogether—have been very difficult decisions. I still feel somewhat guilty and afraid about breaking away. It's hard to be free of that because I've been so connected with the Church.

In addition, I have many unresolved questions about the Church and the Bible. For instance, we're told that we're created in the image of God, but Church teaching often doesn't bear that out. They speak of love but often the emphasis is upon our being unworthy or sinners.

I also wonder whether you, Yeshua, actually said many of the things attributed to you. For example, in the past I believed you were present in the Eucharist,[5] but I wonder about the statement, "Unless you eat my body and drink my blood, you have no life in you."[6] What does that really mean? I've heard you were an Essene[7] and a vegetarian. If so, why did you ask us to eat your body and drink your blood? Maybe the Church made the Eucharist and the host into something other than what you intended.

Were you an Essene from Mount Carmel? Was there a Last Supper? And was Mary Magdalene there? Scripture says that the one Jesus loved was reclining beside him.[8] I'm hoping that was Mary Magdalene.

What happened to Scripture? And why doesn't it include Mother God? Did the Bible get changed at the Council of Nicaea?[9] Suddenly, the Church became powerful, authoritative, and patriarchal, with Mary Magdalene inaccurately depicted as a prostitute. Now Pope Francis says women will never be ordained. Why not?

I understand that you and Mary Magdalene were married. When I heard that, I was so excited and happy. I heard that you both studied in the mystery schools in Egypt. I'm so glad you were together and that Mary supported you and sought you after you were crucified and died. I'm not even sure whether you actually died. Some people say you didn't die.

The fact that you appeared to Mary Magdalene first is so beautiful. Yet when the women ran to tell the apostles, they weren't believed,[10] just like how women still aren't believed so often today.

Before people receive communion in the Catholic Mass, they recite, "I am not worthy to receive you." I think we are worthy because God makes us worthy.

At the end of John's gospel, it says you invited the apostles to come for breakfast. Then you said to Peter, "Do you love me?"[11] I think you said it three times because you wanted Peter to *really* get it. I believe this is the bottom line. It's not about rules or regulations. It's about whether or not we love you.

I don't want to be hard on the Church. Many people find a lot of good in the Church, and so have I.

In the last few years, my wife, Ann, and I have been hearing things we've never heard before. Beautiful things about the world being one—that we're one with the universe and with God. That we're divine. That what we're living is an illusion. That there's no separation. That the reality is we are love.

I want to tell the world about all that we're hearing. I want to tell the Church. And I want to connect with those things myself. I've been praying to be united with the universe, with God, and with you—Yeshua and Mary Magdalene.

I want to raise my intentions and my consciousness to be in Christ consciousness. How can I raise my consciousness? I'm not even sure what Christ consciousness means. Does it mean being Jesus? Being love?

People say to "listen to your heart" because that's where the truth is. I've developed an attitude of listening to others and not to the truth within me. I try to listen to my heart, but nothing seems to happen. How can I find you within me?

I want to *be* love, but it's not easy for me to do. Over the years I've developed a lot of negative feelings. I think things won't work out. I have a feeling of lack. I'm judgmental, and I worry a lot. I don't want to be in doubt when I speak of oneness. I can't prove it, but I still want to say it.

I should give you a chance to speak. I'm sorry for taking so long.

Yeshua: What you have expressed is beautiful. It's also very important to you and to many people in your world. Many people have the same questions, and you've articulated them well.

There's so much we could say about all of this. Your questions, your perception of what's happening in the world, and the changes that are coming—each of those topics is filled with much that we could say and want to say.

Power Versus Love

Yeshua: I have a request of you. I'd like you to ask these questions one at a time, and I want our responses to be made available to the public. You've done an excellent job of clarifying so many questions and concerns, areas where people are torn and long for clarity. People need this information, so they can be free to grow and be supported in that growth. The conflicts you've voiced tend to hold people back. In fact, they were intended to do that.

Your love of the Church is profound. It's also entwined with your love of God, which is very pure. The Church is not pure, so it has confused you in some ways. The Church was created by humans who had their struggles and challenges, which are reflected in the doctrines of the Church.

They used some of what I brought forth to create the Church, but the Church is not what I brought forth. You must be clear about that. Some of what I brought forth can be found in the Bible, but most of the Bible has nothing to do with me.

Do you understand what I am saying?

Tom: I understand that some things in the Bible have nothing to do with you. However, to decipher which things is difficult.

Yeshua: Absolutely. This was the function of the Church, to obfuscate people's relationship to God. People become powerful when they realize their direct relationship to God. The Church was more interested in its own power.

The Church is a structure of the third dimension. More than anything else, the third dimension is a grand exploration of power. Power is an attribute of God, but power separated from God's other attributes creates tremendous suffering. This is what has been created and experienced repeatedly on Earth—even in your religions and churches, not entirely but to a large extent. Religions and churches reflect the third-dimensional consciousness and reality, as do virtually all your institutions in the third dimension.

The third dimension is a place of belief in separation from God. Out of that belief of separation, humans have turned to explore power that's separated from God—power for their own separate survival and wellbeing. This has created your reality in the third dimension, including your religions.

Now is a time of great awakening and transformation into a new reality and consciousness. We often refer to this new reality as the fourth dimension,[12] but the name is not important. You can call it whatever you wish. The reality will not change.

This is the beginning of the realization of which you speak: "The only thing that matters is love. All is love. We are one. We are not separate." This is a tremendous change, and it will not be realized overnight. But the process is underway. It's a great shift out of the third dimension and third-dimensional consciousness.

Some people are very much moving forward into this realization. They are the leaders and helpers of others.

For those who've been connected to God through third-dimensional structures, such as church, this shift might feel like a tearing away of the old. The parts of those structures that aren't supporting their relationship to God are being released. Yet it is still true that parts of religions and churches *were* helping people to connect to God. This can be very confusing for people who have connected to God through churches and traditional religious organizations. Now they have to separate out what was real and true from what was imposed and was not part of the true path, perhaps blocking or obscuring the true path. It's like separating the wheat from the chaff.

This task is very important and real for you and for many others. You are in a unique position because of your strong commitment to connecting with God through your life, energy, awareness, and actions. You followed through on that by taking dedicated steps, such as becoming a priest and then letting go of the priesthood. Both choices put you into a position of great depth and awareness. That position is one that other people can relate to, with its attendant questions, struggles, and challenges, because they have the same ones. They trust you because of your choices in life and your experiences. People trust your purity, authenticity, and realness.

People can feel your heart, which is well developed. That's a wonderful thing.

Yet you still have questions. How to resolve what you've been told? How to feel even more from your heart? How to be in your heart? How to resolve and align long-held beliefs with what you're feeling and sensing now and what your heart is opening to?

Is that correct?

Tom: Yes.

Yeshua: We ask you to help others by going into these questions you've raised and allowing us to respond to them one by one. Are you open to doing this as a form of service to others?

Tom: Yes, I am. But I don't know how I can do that.

Yeshua: Mercedes can help you. She's very good at these things.

Tom: I've been asked to give a talk at an interdenominational retreat. I've been thinking about which passages from the Bible I can use for that talk.

Yeshua: You must understand that the majority of people who will be open to what you have to say won't be found in churches.

Tom: Yes.

Yeshua: Everyone is supported in their own way in their growth and what is right for them. For those participating in churches, their participation is, by and large, supporting their soul growth and soul work. It is never anyone's place to tell someone else what to believe. But there are those who will be hungry for what you have to share. It's simply that, most likely, they will not be found in churches.

Tom: I've thought about that too.

Yeshua: I had the same experience when I incarnated.

The Indoctrination of Right and Wrong

Yeshua: So, how can we help you? Obviously, your questions are all important and valuable, and we want to answer them. But on a personal level, what would be most supportive for you?

Tom: I guess to know that I'm on the right path and that leaving the Church wouldn't be the end of the world. To know that I can listen to my heart and know which way to go. Am I doing the right thing? I feel some guilt in it.

Yeshua: You have been taught guilt. This is part of Church teaching and the program of control the Church uses over people. You can choose. Do you want to continue to be part of the program of guilt, or do you want to let go of it?

Tom: I would sooner let go of it.

Yeshua: I support that choice.

Part of the way people have been controlled in the third dimension is that they've been indoctrinated to believe in right and wrong. In the fourth dimension, you realize right and wrong were simply a program of control that was taught to you and that you agreed to abide by. You realize there isn't an *external truth* to rightness and wrongness.

It's like a child. A child hears its parents say, "Do this—this is the right thing. Don't do that—that's the wrong thing." These dictates are often followed by rewards or punishments. It's unfortunate that parents teach these ideas of right and wrong to their children, reinforced through rewards and punishments. They're simply passing on what they learned and believe is the case. This is how reality is maintained.

In fact, there is no rightness and wrongness. That's not to say that things don't affect you. Things always affect you. But the effect is not in terms of right and wrong. The effect is much more practical. Something might hurt or help you. Move you toward or away from love. Move you into connecting with God or away from God. That is the effect.

The effect is never rightness or wrongness. Judgments of right or wrong are simply programs of control.

Guilt is about believing you have done something wrong. Do you see how effective guilt is at controlling you? If you can be convinced that you've done something wrong, then whoever is determining what's right and wrong has tremendous control over you.

If we take the wrongness and rightness out, what are you left with if you leave the Church?

Tom: Choice.

Yeshua: Yes. And freedom. You can choose to leave. In the next moment, you can choose not to leave and to go back to where you were. You can choose to leave again. You can choose infinitely.

Choice and free will are two great gifts of the third dimension. They are two of the greatest blessings available.

You can choose to explore and follow your heart—to grow in living from your heart and to free yourself from obstacles in doing so. Indeed, you are already on this path, but your beliefs are causing you conflict.

You must also look at other repercussions of leaving the Church. Again, if you take away right and wrong, you probably feel grief at leaving behind what has been your "home" for a good deal of your life. That home has brought you blessings as well as challenges and difficulties—it hasn't been black or white. Your family of origin is also very connected with the Church. To leave might affect your family relationships. Ideally it wouldn't, but it may. So, that's very real too.

To accept that you're affected by your experiences is part of being connected to God. To be truly connected to God is to be connected to the wholeness of your experience—the choice, the freedom, the beauty, the sadness, the possible loss or gain—*all* of it. Connecting to the whole of your experience will support you in being in your heart and being alive.

Your higher self already knows what is right for you. Your higher self is your direct connection to God. This is what the Church is most afraid of. Rules of rightness and wrongness are designed to divorce you from your higher self. But your higher self already knows what is right for you. What's right for you is different from ultimate rightness. It simply means what your soul is calling you to.

Can you feel this?

Tom: I feel a bit of anxiety as I think about what you're saying.

Yeshua: What is the anxiety?

Tom: I worry what people will think of me.

Yeshua: Yes. This is important. It's part of your humanity, part of love, to be connected to others. What others think of you matters. The thoughts you have of one another affect each and every one of you. Certainly, you have experienced being affected by others' thoughts, yes?

Tom: Yes.

Yeshua: So, this is real, not something to be dismissed with self-judgments, such as, *I shouldn't care what others think of me. I should be beyond that. I should be stronger.* That's denying your humanity. If you deny your humanity, you deny your heart. You deny the reality of love.

Human beings are tender, vulnerable. You don't want to deny that. Humans *do* care about others' connection to them, which includes others' thoughts about them.

Some may think terrible thoughts about you. That's a reflection of them and their spiritual path; it's not about you. Whatever someone thinks is the food they're feeding themselves. They can try to give it to you, but you don't have to take it in. It's simply a reflection of their consciousness, their moment on their spiritual path.

The greater question is, what will you think of those who think such thoughts of you? Your response to this question reflects your spiritual path.

I could not have done what I did had I been concerned with what people thought of me. Many people thought terrible things about me. That was their spiritual path.

It takes strength of heart to stand in that fire, to care more about your heart and your true connection to God than other people's fears. It takes strength of heart to allow others their fear and still love them, if that love is true for you. Their greatest fear is that they may be just like you. If you can see this, it's easy to love them. Just as you have fear in taking this step, they have the same fear.

What is in your heart now?

Tom: It's consoling to hear what you said. I can experience and visualize you taking your stand, being in the garden. Scripture says you sweat blood and tears[13] because you stood for what you had to stand for. Everybody seemed to be against you.

Yeshua: Yes, and that is the moment you're always in. Do you stand in love, or do you absorb the fear of others and return it in fear?

Choosing love does not mean you are fearless. That is a misunderstanding. You give the fear to God and let God direct you. You do not have to be fearless. You simply do not return the fear to others.

Tom: I guess I have to listen to my heart and know that I am really hearing God and not put my power in the Church or in others.

Yeshua: Listening to your heart is the greatest step in transitioning into the next dimension. The truth has always resided in your heart; it's where your power is—the power of your connection to God.

I have tears of joy and welcome in hearing you say this, for you are my spiritual brother. We are not different. We are not separate. I came to help others by showing them the path they would travel, not to show my own difference. I couldn't do that. I am not different. Perhaps just further down the path is all.

I welcome you. I reach out to you. I extend my hand and my embrace.

Tom: Thank you.

Yeshua: Absolutely.

Mary Magdalene

Tom: I love you, and I love Mary Magdalene. Was Mary Magdalene at the Last Supper?

Yeshua: Of course! [laughs] Why would I not have my beloved at my side?

Mary was more than simply a follower. Mary is my divine partner. Mary came to bring the Feminine, just as I came to bring the Masculine.[14] The Church has cut out this part of what we did and what our work was because they were afraid. But it is coming forth now. We knew this would happen. We understood. And we're glad it's finally time for everyone to have access to the whole of what we brought forth: the Masculine and the Feminine. Both of us were revealing, teaching, and supporting—together. So of course, she was there.

Tom: I learned a lot of this from my wife. She is so good.

Yeshua: You are very wise. So many men need this understanding and valuing of the Feminine. Women have moved ahead because it's more natural for them to receive the Feminine. They're receiving this understanding of the Feminine first, by and large, and men are receiving it through the women. This is the first stage. You are very blessed to have your wife and to receive her in the way you do.

Tom: Yesterday, at the equinox, I was praying for the whole of creation to rise, something we're calling ascension.[15] Then this morning as I was praying, it felt like a sexual union inside of me. Could that be God touching me?

Yeshua: Absolutely! This is another aspect of the Feminine that the Church doesn't want people to connect with and understand. As you move into the fourth dimension, you'll see that dimension is very sexual in the *true* form of sexual union because the Masculine and Feminine are always in union with each other.

One aspect of the separation that beings in the third dimension experience is the separation of the Masculine and the Feminine. This relationship is being healed and shifted back into its higher form by reuniting the Masculine and the Feminine.

Tom: I can go back to that feeling of sexual union inside me when I'm trying to search for God.

Yeshua: Yes. It's a gift and a blessing. Is there more that's in your heart right now?

Tom: There's more joy.

Yeshua: [laughs] That is your sign. Let joy be your guide.

Tom: I guess I'll still give my talk at the retreat, but I'll try to be careful.

Yeshua: Ask your heart, and give the talk for yourself. Let the talk come from what your heart wants to say rather than from your mind trying to figure out the right thing to say. Let your heart guide you. Be connected through your heart to your higher self, to hear what you feel called to say.

There is a reason why you are before this group of people. You don't even need to understand—just let it flow through you. Let yourself be the conduit of this connection to God. Let that be your prayer: that you may support whatever is meant to happen, whatever is most beneficial at that moment. Certainly, you can call upon me and Mary.

Tom: I'll let the two of you speak.

Yeshua: [chuckling] We are happy to do that.

One of the most valuable ways of supporting people is to share your story. And not just the "good news"—the part you think looks good and supports you. Share the *real* story, whatever it is. Even the parts that aren't resolved, that you don't yet know the answer to. That is completely fine. What people are fed by is your authenticity. You have much to share that can help people.

Tom: Thank you very much.

Yeshua: You are welcome. I am sensing this is a completion point for today. Does it feel that way to you also?

Tom: I have one last question. Were you an Essene from Mount Carmel?

Yeshua: I was many things. I was definitely part of the Essene community. And the Essenes were a great help to me on many levels and at different periods. But I wasn't only an Essene. I was guided in many traditions, schools, and paths, so I would be prepared to serve most fully.

Tom: Were you incarnated many times or just that one time?

Yeshua: Just that one time.

Tom: Thank you for coming the one time.

Yeshua: You are welcome.

Tom: Thank you for showing us who we really are.

Yeshua: Yes. We are all God. That is the truth.

Tom: There is nowhere to go.

Yeshua: [chuckling] No need.

Non-separation from God

Yeshua: There is one more thing I wish to share. In the beginning of our session today, you referred to all of this being an illusion. I want to clarify that the illusion is that you are separate from God or separate from anything. Everything is God, so either way of saying it is the same thing.

What's not an illusion is your experience. The illusion is that your experience isn't God, that you are somehow separate from God. Out of that comes all fear and worry, based on the illusion of separation. Fear and worry are also real. The manifestation is real, all of it. It's the beautiful flowering of God's essence. The only illusion is that you are separate.

For most humans, this awareness of non-separation will evolve. Your knowingness that you're not separate will come, step by step, as you realize this truth, and that is a wonderful thing.

So, now I feel complete for today.

Tom: Thank you for clarifying that understanding of illusion. It's really important for me.

Yeshua: You can give yourself fully to every moment. Whatever is appearing in every moment is the fullness of God. Do not let the idea of illusion become another reason to separate yourself. Whatever is appearing is a gift for you in this moment. Receive the gift.

Tom: Thank you.

Yeshua: You are welcome, my brother. I love you tremendously.

Tom: I embrace you and Mary. And Mercedes.

Yeshua: Thank you so much. Continue to let your light shine so brightly. We love you.

Tom: I love you too. Thank you.

.

THREE

Understanding the Third Dimension

[Eleven months after the initial session]

Yeshua: Greetings, brother. This is Yeshua. I'm very happy to be with you in this form once again.

Thank you for responding to my request and for your openness to doing what I've asked. Thank you for your willingness to ask these questions in a public forum. Even that is a step of courage, which will support many. Thank you so much.

I want you to know that Mary Magdalene is available at any time if it feels to her or to me that her participation would be helpful, but at this point I am responding.

Tom: Thank you, Yeshua, thank you.

Yeshua: You are so welcome. I love you so much.

Tom: Thank you for taking the time to speak with me. I have written my questions on paper, so I stay on track. Is that OK?

Yeshua: Absolutely. I'm completely fine with whatever feels comfortable and supportive to you.

Tom: Over the years I've had many questions about the Bible and its truth. Consequently, I've had questions about you—why you came and what you taught. I question and have many mixed feelings about the Roman Catholic Church and whether I should stay in the Church.

At the same time, a tsunami of information is coming in from various sources, beautiful things about how humanity is awakening and how our world is being transformed, and challenging things, such as the idea that humans have been controlled for eons in all facets of life. I wonder about the cosmos, the universe, and the existence of other beings (ETs), and all this brings up more questions.

For the most part, my journey has been an interior one. But I didn't trust myself. I can't overestimate the power I've given over to the Church throughout my life and to others who I thought were more intelligent—theologians, biblical scholars, and the like.

When you asked me to share my questions in a public forum, I agreed. However, there's a hesitancy in me. *Why me? There are many others who could do a better job than me, others who would have better questions and have thought this through in a deeper way. Others who are more eloquent than I am.*

I've also had an embarrassing feeling that, in reading this, others might say, "These questions are juvenile. He should know the answers." I don't want my hesitancy to hold me back. Knowing that you asked me to do this, especially for others, makes me want to do it.

My entire quest in life thus far has been to find the truth, so I may experience true freedom. That's why I became a priest. In asking these questions, I want to be of service to others and to myself in moving from confusion to clarity, from uncertainty to truth, and from frustration to freedom and joy.

And so, with gratitude to you, Mary, and Mercedes, I'm responding to your request. Thank you so much for inviting me to do this.

Authority and Power

Tom: I want to begin with the Hebrew Scriptures. How and why were they written?

Yeshua: What do you think? [There is a pause, and then Tom laughs.] And why do you ask?

Tom: The Hebrew Scriptures are at the root of Christianity, so they must be important. I imagine they were written by the people who lived at the time they were written.

Yeshua: Are you asking if you should believe what is written in the Old Testament? Is this your real question?

Tom: I guess so. I'm wondering how true it all is. Everybody else is following the Scriptures, so they seem to be true.

Yeshua: I would suggest that it's not accurate to say that everyone else is following the Scriptures. Perhaps in your realm of association, throughout your life, it may have seemed that way. I would say a great many people are not following the Scriptures.

Tom: Hmm . . .

Yeshua: This is the first principle: You have the power to choose.

Whether you're looking at the Old Testament or the New Testament, the Bible is not the word of God that was somehow transmitted to only some beings while carrying the rules and laws for all people. Yet, by and large, your churches have presented the Bible that way. Would you say that's accurate?

Tom: Yes, that's right. Very accurate.

Yeshua: This is a reflection of third-dimensional consciousness. Third-dimensional consciousness is rooted in power structures, which are based on "authority-over." The structures establish authority, and that authority wields power over others.

The Christian Church has been a major structure of the Western world. Before that there was the Jewish religion. Both were based in authority, and the authority was established in a book. Where do you think this book came from? Me? God?

Tom: I think it came from the writers.

Yeshua: Exactly. But in the third dimension, that's a disappointment [laughs]. *What kind of authority does that have? That's just some other person just like me!* [Yeshua continues to laugh, and Tom chuckles.]

Some person said, "I know how to play this game. I'm going to claim *real* authority here. I'm going to claim this came from God, and I'm going to convince others that that's so. Based on that, they'll need to adhere to what's in here. What's more, I'm going to decide what's in there!" [Yeshua laughs boisterously.]

You know very well that's what happened, certainly with the New Testament. A group of people got together and decided what would be in the Bible and what would not be in the Bible. You're aware of this, yes?

Tom: Yes.

Yeshua: Yet human beings don't want to perceive it that way because another major aspect of the third dimension is fear. Previously, we spoke about the third dimension being rooted in disconnection from the divine. The ultimate disconnection appears to be death. In the third dimension, there's a constant struggle against something that's going to get you. That leads to striving for power, which will save you from the thing that's going to get you. You can sum up the whole experience of the third dimension in this way.

Tom: I can relate to that! [laughs]

Yeshua: Everyone in the third dimension can relate to that. It's the fundamental field you're all dealing with—or avoiding dealing with. But it's there nonetheless, a longing to align yourself with some ultimate authority or power that can save you from the sense that something is trying to get you. It's a feeling that you're not safe; at any time you can be snuffed out.

Out of that feeling, people have made choices to ignore what they know. People ignore that it was a group of humans who got together and said, "This is going to be the Bible. We're going to say *this* is the word of God, and the *other books* aren't the word of God. And here it is."

These religious books, and all forms of authority, are a response to that deeper fear that tends to run human beings in the third dimension. They manipulate and thrive on that fear.

This is not to say that there's *nothing* in those books that may have actually happened or that may be aligned with supportive beliefs for individuals. It's just to say that what's presented is not the ultimate authority of God, which must then be adhered to—or else what's going to happen to you is going to be even worse than in the third dimension! [laughs] You're going to go to hell, where it's going to be even worse than here, worse than you can imagine, the ultimate fear! This was promoted too. Is that accurate?

Tom: Yes, it sure was.

Yeshua: So the flames of fear were fanned. It's a cycle that goes on and on. Promote the fear, then promote the authority that's based on the fear, and then sustain the authority through promoting more fear. That's a hallmark of the third dimension.

Those of you who are incarnated in the third dimension came here to learn about power, authority, and fear. This third-dimensional structure has supported your learning. It has also supported your growth beyond power, authority, and fear. It has supported many things and perhaps limited many things. Ultimately, if you're involved in the third dimension and its structures, your soul has chosen them for its learning.

At a certain point, your learning will be complete in that form, and you will begin to choose other forms. It sounds like that's what's happened in your case. And part of you is wondering, *What about that old form? What about all those things I thought were true?* Now you're starting to see them through a different lens.

Tom: Yes. Hearing you speak and thinking about the questions I have, I'm telling myself, *I might as well throw them away, and let's just go to Timmy's Restaurant for coffee.* [Tom and Yeshua laugh.]

How Creation Happens

Tom: My next question is, how would you describe Creation? What would you say about the Creation story in the Hebrew Bible?

Yeshua: Again, this is one possible story that was created by people. Not by God, by people. There are many, many stories. If you look around the world and study, you can easily come up with *many* stories. Different cultures have different stories.

Tom: And they're all good stories.

Yeshua: They're great stories! And it's possible that all of them are true. It's possible that all of them are based on real experiences people had.

As you go beyond the third dimension, you start to understand that beings are always creating their reality. And beings don't necessarily create the same reality. They create the reality that reflects their consciousness and what their souls want to experience.

Usually, at this point people ask, "Are you saying people who are suffering created that themselves?" The answer is yes. This is not an uncompassionate answer. It's not saying, "If they created their circumstances, then they should just accept the consequences. It has nothing to do with me." It's not true that their reality has nothing to do with you because you somehow created them to be in your life. So, it has everything to do with you as well. Does that make sense?

Tom: Yes, it does. I've been learning more and more that the world mirrors back what we're thinking and intending.

Yeshua: Absolutely. And there can be many, many realities. The idea that we're all existing in the same reality is one of the humorous jokes, you might say, of the third dimension [laughs]. If you have a conversation with your spouse, you might be aware of this. [Yeshua and Tom laugh.]

Tom: I'm hearing that we live parallel lives, and there are different dimensions. We can move from one to the other. It's beyond what I've been taught.

Yeshua: Absolutely. This is the higher-dimensional understanding and reality that you're *not* taught in the third dimension. You're taught the third-dimensional point of view, that life somehow began with the physical, and there must be an explanation for physical creation. You have all these stories, which may align with actual events. Perhaps they were creation events or not—in the sense you're thinking of as the ultimate creation. But the stories serve various third-dimensional purposes—such as coming to peace, being in trust, or accepting life. To the extent that those aspects of your being are fulfilled by the story, you will likely accept that story. Doing so will support what *you* came to do, what your soul wants to accomplish.

When your soul is complete with the aspects of your soul work that the story fulfilled, and you are ready to accomplish other things, the story will no longer be a match for your consciousness. Then you will let go of that story and find different stories, experiences, and realities. You could think of it as going to a movie. Most people have had the experience while watching a movie where they temporarily forget their own life and reality. The movie becomes real. Then the movie ends, and they think, *Oh, it was just a movie.*

You might think of your life that way. This is one movie playing out, being projected as real, or seemingly real. You are all the parts of the movie [Yeshua laughs], being projected into what seems like reality.

Tom: If we enjoy the drama, we stay in it. If not, we choose something else.

Yeshua: Yes. When you lose interest in the drama, when it's no longer a match for who you are and what your soul wants, why watch that movie? It's not interesting. Others may find that movie interesting. There's no judgment about who's better or worse, higher or lower. Different souls have different purposes and soul needs.

Tom: The way you express this is so freeing. I haven't lived that freely.

Yeshua: That's part of the third dimension. When you feel you're in danger, and your life is based on fear, you often have tunnel vision due to your need for survival. Out of that survival drive, you look for the authority that will support you. Then you sign up, "lock, stock, and barrel," as they say, for whatever's involved in getting the goods of that authority. Generally, this requires belief in this or that principle or that you must do certain things that somehow support the authority. Often it involves giving your power to the authority.

When you break out of that, suddenly, you're calling your power back. You have power you didn't know you had. You have the power to choose. Once again, we return to the principle of choice.

Authorities don't like you to know you have the power to choose. They want you to think you only have the choice they're offering. Otherwise, your alternative is death, or at least great risk. That's part of their agenda to support their authority.

Tom: When it comes to creation, I suppose we've chosen to be who we are.

Yeshua: Yes.

The Bigger Picture

Yeshua: Let me say one more thing about this. From the third-dimensional point of view, the question of creation is very important. Physicality seems to have a beginning and an end. Then the questions arise: "How did it begin? Was there something before the beginning?" [chuckles] "How is it going to end, and what's going to happen after the ending?" These questions seem pertinent from the point of view that all that's real is this physically based reality.

From a different perspective, the field becomes so wide that those questions are like a dot, a point that disappears into the vista of ongoing-ness. You didn't just begin. Even if there's reincarnation, it's not just about this physical reality or the third dimension. You're in a vast process that I would describe as ultimately coming from pure Source.

Pure Source is not manifest in any dimension. It's beyond manifestation, prior to manifestation. You could call this pure Source by many names. One name is God.

Out of this pure Source, a desire arose to know itself *in form*. This may be what you call creation. I tend to use different words because creation tends to be connected for many with Christianity and Christian beliefs, which seem like a great limitation to me. I prefer the words "manifestation," "incarnation," and "coming into form."

This coming into form was the beginning of the creation of dimensions. The first step away from the formlessness of pure Source was the formation of Mother-Father God. Unfortunately, Christianity and some other religions don't want you to know about Mother God. They've restricted God to the Masculine. But that is not the case.

Then there were further manifestations from there. You might think of the emergence of Mother-Father God as similar to the birth of a new being, which starts with the union of the sperm and the egg. Then there's continued creation from there. Two cells divide to become four cells and on and on. That's how you might look at the creation of the dimensions and beings in those dimensions.

Within that creation, the third dimension and human beings are just a dot. It's like seeing pictures of Earth in the context of the solar system, the galaxy, other galaxies, the universe, the multiverse, and on and on. You see how big Earth is in the midst of that larger context [laughs]. That's similar to what human beings are in the third dimension. But they are not unimportant! You are quite significant! Human beings have a vital role in the cosmos. That's why so many beings are here helping you.

Tom: I understand that many beings are watching and seeing how we're doing on our journey of evolution. They're here to help us.

Yeshua: More than watching! Many have the soul function of supporting in many ways. I am one of those.

Tom: You came and are still here.

Yeshua: And still involved. Still having conversations like these. But I'm doing more than just communicating. I'm involved in the physics, the energetics of what's being created and chosen on Earth.

Tom: Thank you so much for these responses. It's so heartening.

Yeshua: Is this addressing your questions?

Tom: Yes.

You Are God

Tom: Here's my next question. The Hebrew Scriptures speak of how humanity is created in the image and likeness of God. I've heard that we've been given God's power as well. What do these ideas mean?

Yeshua: These questions are based on being separate from God.

Tom: Yes.

Yeshua: If you're not separate from God, if you are God, whose image are you going to have? [laughs]

You don't need to be *like* God. You *are* God! You are God in human form, manifest in the third-dimensional plane on Earth. You're in the process of discovering who you are—which is really the process of remembering, waking up, coming out of that movie theater.

Tom: I'm trying to be in that oneness with God, but it's really difficult for me to say "I am God."

Yeshua: Yes, because this is not just a belief or a good idea to which you can say, "OK, I sign up" [laughs]. "I'm pledging to this idea." It's got to be the core of your being, *who you are*, that knows this. That's an awakening, which is often called a "realization." It's not something you can believe yourself into.

This is why people engage in traditional spiritual practices, such as meditation and prayer, to support this awakening. People are also beginning to access other higher-dimensional forms of connecting with their God-self. The next dimension (the fourth dimension) is based in the etheric and astral bodies and planes.[16] There are practices in those arenas where people can also know their God-self through etheric and astral-based practices.

Awakening is a real transformation. You know it when you go through it. It's not simply a belief or even an experience. People have experiences that are very real, where for a period of time they know their connection to God through that experience. It's like a wonderful dream or a great meditation, a shamanic journey. What makes it an experience is that it ends [laughs]. Then you return to your prior state of consciousness, where you didn't feel that sense of connection.

An awakening doesn't go away. It becomes your new state and identity, who you are at your core. It's not something you strive to do, remember, or ascribe to. It simply is how you know yourself to be.

This is why people do spiritual practices, because these practices support these transformations and awakenings. *Some* individuals have these awakenings spontaneously. Often these are individuals who've done spiritual practice in previous lifetimes. They're drawing upon a reservoir that their soul carries, which supports them in their awakening. If awakening hasn't occurred for you, and you're longing for it, wanting it, then spiritual experiences feed your longing and give you the motivation to practice.

Tom: Thank you.

Adam and Eve

Tom: Should I continue asking questions?

Yeshua: As they seem real for you. Even if you think, *Perhaps this is silly*, it might still be valuable to ask the question; something may come out of it that's supportive and helpful.

Tom: What really happened in the story of Adam and Eve? Did we fall from grace? Did we choose to live as if we were separated from God? Why did we make that choice? And how did it impact our history? You've kind of answered this already.

Yeshua: How would you answer it now, hearing what I've said?

Tom: Well, we chose to learn certain things. We came to Earth and the third dimension to learn through these experiences.

Yeshua: Yes. Exactly. There was a period of time, in your life where aligning yourself with the beliefs and ideas from the Garden of Eden story was valuable for you. Then, over time, you noticed limitations that became less and less acceptable to you. Is that accurate?

Tom: That's right. Yes.

Yeshua: I have an analogy that might be helpful. I have a concern about saying this because people might take it in a judgmental way, and that isn't the way I mean it. But think of the story of Santa Claus. Many parents tell their children this story when they're young, and it supports something beautiful. It supports the children in feeling loved and also in feeling they live in a magical realm. The story has also been used somewhat manipulatively by communicating to children that they must be good—and if they're bad, they won't get presents. But in its most benign form, the Santa Claus story supports children in experiencing love and magic in manifestation.

As children grow and become older children and adults, to still believe in Santa Claus, to still believe they're going to receive love and experience the magic of the universe in that particular form, becomes a limit. Most children grow beyond this story at a certain age, even during childhood. It's a natural process. Do we have to get rid of Santa Claus? Not necessarily. But perhaps we don't want adults to believe in Santa Claus. That may not be supportive.

The reason I hesitated to give this analogy is because you could say, "Believing in Santa Claus is immature and juvenile." I heard you use that term in reference to yourself earlier, when suggesting that some of your questions may be judged as immature. You implied that to go beyond them would be mature and somehow better or superior.

This is another limit of third-dimensional thinking, to be constantly ranking things as better/worse, higher/lower, good/bad, mature/immature, all of that. There are endless ways of doing this stratification and ranking. It's a way of trying to have power by being higher in the ranking rather than lower [laughs]. As you go beyond third-dimensional thinking and the limitation of what is often referred to as "duality," you will see the perfection of all different experiences. There's no need to rank them as higher/lower, good/bad. They either serve and support or they don't.

Tom: Thank you. Actually, I think I can answer the next couple of questions.

Yeshua: [laughs] Wonderful! I like having a dialogue with you! [laughs again]

Tom: Do the Scriptures tell us how God interacted with people, or are they an interpretation by the writers as to how God was relating to people? In the Hebrew Scriptures, quite often God is depicted as angry, choosing sides in wars, and wanting to "get even" when things didn't go his way. Please speak about this. I think the writers were intending to manipulate people by saying that God was going to get them if they didn't listen to what the writers were saying.

Yeshua: Yes. Some people believe God created humans in His/Her likeness, and others believe humans created God in their likeness.

Tom: [laughs] Yes.

Yeshua: Again, if humans are God, that's sort of a moot point. However, I would say there's a kernel of truth in both.

Beings create their reality, including their stories and beliefs, as a mirror of their consciousness. Stories that depict God as angry, vengeful, and using power to destroy people if they don't do what God wants—you could say all of these reflect the consciousness of the people who created those stories, as well as those who disseminate and adhere to those stories. Doing so has supported their exploration of that aspect of power. As long as the story is helping their consciousness grow, they'll continue to create, support, or adhere to it. When their consciousness shifts or changes, the story is no longer valuable; it loses its interest and its hold on them..

Tom: I think the story of a God who's angry is losing its value.

Yeshua: For many, yes. Your world is changing. Many are in the midst of a profound shift beyond third-dimensional consciousness into the fourth dimension and beyond. For people making this shift, the story of an angry God is losing its potency and interest.

In your world today, there's a kind of struggle. You could even call it a war between the people who are still adhering to third-dimensional consciousness and the people who are shifting into a different consciousness. They're not matched. They're not having the same experience or wanting the same things. It's creating a certain level of conflict in your world.

But you could also see it a different way. You could see this conflict as a birth process where a new kind of cell division is going on, creating those who are ready to shift into a different consciousness and reality. Just as the birth process often involves pain, there can be a certain pain in that division.

Tom: I think the world is experiencing that. More and more people are loving rather than hating. They want more love to come into the world, and they are working hard to make that so.

Yeshua: Yes. Some of your leaders, the pioneers, have spoken to this. "When the power of love replaces the love of power, the world will know peace."[17] This is what you're seeing.

The Nature of Truth

Tom: How accurate are the Hebrew Scriptures? Did God select the Israelites as the chosen people? Are those people now the Jews? (I suppose I could answer these questions too.)

Yeshua: Here we get into a different kind of power in the third dimension, the authority of the mind and of knowing. The authority of *the truth*. In the third dimension, this has been one of the ways people have claimed authority. "*I* have the truth" or "*We* have the truth." Within that, the truth can include things like "We are the chosen people" or "Whatever we want to say the truth is, that's what it is." Then there can be clashes: "Your truth is the wrong truth! Our truth is the right truth!" and "We're entitled to kill you because your truth is wrong!" [laughs] This is all part of the third-dimensional movie, the underlying structure, the grid work that supports the third dimension.

But what if there isn't *one* truth? What if there isn't one reality? What if knowing the truth doesn't give you power over others? What if that truth is only *your* truth and doesn't tell you anything about others? And it is only your truth right now—truth meaning what aligns for you in your whole being. Truth doesn't necessarily refer to the mind because it's in greater alignment when it aligns with your heart. It's in greater alignment still when it aligns with your soul.

Your rational, thinking, knowing mind is a superficial part of yourself. There's a much deeper part of the mind that's much more profound. But in general, this deeper part is cloaked by the rational, thinking mind. And in the third dimension, the rational, thinking mind tends to be in service to power and authority.

Some other part of your being is going to start to become strong. For many, it will be their heart. They will start to trust the authority of the heart as opposed to the mind. It's not that the heart is going to say, "I'm the authority now. You must be subservient to me or you must not exist. I'm the *only* authority that can be." Heart authority is not of that nature. Heart authority is inclusive. Heart authority welcomes the mind to serve in its true function of supporting with information and choice. This is how you'll start to shift into the higher dimensions.

Tom: By listening to the heart.

Yeshua: Yes. You might ask, "How do I listen to the heart?"

Tom: Yes, I ask that question.

Yeshua: [laughs] This is so much of the work that my beloved, Mary Magdalene, has brought forth. The heart, in general, is the Feminine part of your being, regardless of whether you're a man, woman, or whatever gender you identify with. You all have the Feminine part. If you prefer, you can call it the "yin" part, in the Eastern understanding of yin-yang. It doesn't matter how you label it. Yet there's something valuable about labeling it "the Feminine" because most in the third dimension have resistance to the Feminine. You even have resistance to acknowledging you have resistance! [laughs] This is coming up a lot in your world today.

My beloved Mary Magdalene is perfectly equipped to support humanity at this time with this very process for opening, empowering, and strengthening the heart. She has taught this—which includes teaching the foundation that allows the heart to open, through your body, sexuality, and emotions.

Most of you who are more connected to your Masculine part—which is, in its simplest form, your mind—don't want to hear about the Feminine. You don't want to hear about your body, sexuality, and emotions. You brush it off. You believe, *I've already dealt with that. I don't need that. I've got that under control.* And you're fascinated by your mind. This is part of the fear of the Feminine, which the Masculine is unwilling even to acknowledge, let alone begin to open to. It's part of the foundational fear of the third dimension, which must be addressed and changed before you're ready to go beyond the third dimension.

Tom: I have questions about all the abuse that's happening in our world and in our churches. Unless we incorporate the Feminine, we'll never address this abuse.

Yeshua: The abuse is just now coming to light. It's been going on for centuries or longer. But only now is the consciousness awakened and developed enough to allow it to come to light and be exposed.

The Masculine is so afraid to give over its domination of the Feminine. The Masculine has dominated through many forms. One form has been domination through denial—denial that abuse exists and is happening, denial that it's wrong or hurting people, denial that it should change. Denial in any form.

The Masculine is very afraid of the Feminine. This fear is at the root of so many of the problems in your world. It's also part of what's coming to light, so it may begin to change and allow you to evolve beyond this painful place of the third dimension.

Tom: I thank my wife for so often helping me move beyond that fear.

Yeshua: Absolutely! Many are coming to understand that the Feminine is going to lead at this time. It isn't a leading of authority or power over. It's leading through love, which will start to attract the Masculine to open to the Feminine. *Through love.* It's the only way.

Tom: Lately, we've been told to let go of beliefs that no longer serve us. Returning to my question about the Jews being God's chosen people, I've got to let go of that.

Yeshua: This is more of the Masculine agenda. *My mind has been believing this, but this is wrong. Therefore, my mind needs to change and believe something else. And I need to "power through" to make that happen* [laughs]. You can do that if you want, but it won't necessarily liberate you. It will just replace one belief with another set of beliefs, based on the same consciousness.

Or you can choose to do something else. You can choose to listen to your being. You can start to listen to your body, emotions, sexuality, and heart and then follow *your* authority. Part of that authority means asking, *What beliefs are true for me? Which are aligned with my being and my experience? What is my truth?*

You can certainly be informed by the beliefs, experiences, and reports of others, but don't give your power to them. Don't set them up to be the authority and in the process give your power away. Choose to be *your own* authority.

Maintain a state of awareness of yourself and your reality based in your Feminine *and* Masculine. Include all the Feminine parts of yourself—body, emotion, energy, sexuality, heart—as well as your mind. As things shift, and your beliefs no longer fit, and new beliefs become a fit—through all this, you will become fluid rather than rigid and stuck.

Tom: In the past that's where I've been quite unfree. I haven't honored the authority within me. I've given my authority to others, especially the Church.

Yeshua: Yes. They had no interest in empowering you. If you became empowered, they would lose their power—at least power in the way it's been set up, as *power-over* and authority *versus* submission.

So, you weren't supported, but you found your way. Some part of your being was guiding you elsewhere. Congratulations! Well done!

Tom: I have one more question from the Hebrew Scriptures, but I suppose it's not a valid question either! [Yeshua and Tom laugh.] You're tipping over all my sacred cows! [Tom and Yeshua laugh again.] Can you tell us about King David? Are you from the line of King David?

Yeshua: What does it matter?

Tom: I guess it doesn't matter.

Yeshua: [laughs] Do I need to be from King David for you to accept what I'm offering you as valuable to your growth and your soul?

Tom: No, you don't have to be from the line of King David.

Yeshua: But if you restrict yourself to your mind, if you cut off the Feminine parts of yourself, you might need that. Do you see how restrictive that is, how flimsy it is to base your life on the mind?

If you open to these other parts of yourself—which ultimately opens you to your heart and to the uniting of your heart with your sacred mind—you don't need to base your authority on a lineage from any king or historical person. You base your authority on what is in your soul and what your soul is telling you. That may involve choosing to align with certain things, systems, or beliefs or choosing to align with some of them, parts of them, whatever. At that point you become empowered to create what is right for you. You claim your birthright as a God-being. Part of that birthright is that you are a creator.

You ask, "What is creation?" This moment is creation. Every moment is creation if you claim your God-nature and God-being and assume your power to create. Even if you don't, you're always creating. You're simply doing so unconsciously. Welcome to creation! What movie shall we go to today? [Tom laughs.]

From Fear to Joy

Tom: Is there anything else you'd like to say about the Hebrew Scriptures?

Yeshua: As you move out of this movie of the third dimension, which is rooted in fear, your life will start to be based in joy. One thing you can ask yourself as a measure of this shift is, *When I align to these ideas or texts, does it increase my joy?* That may be one form of discerning whether it's supporting you or not. This question is much more important than "Is it true?" What is your experience?

Tom: Just being a part of this dialogue with you brings me joy. When we completed the last conversation, I was filled with joy.

A few days ago during meditation, the words "gift of God" came to me. I wondered, *What does "gift of God" mean?* Then the words came: *If only you knew the gift of God.* It reminded me of the Scripture passage where Jesus said to the Samaritan woman, "If only you knew the gift of God, you'd be asking me for a drink and I would give you living water."[18] I had been struggling so much with my questions and wondering if I should ask them. I realized at that moment that your request for me to ask these questions was a gift to me. I never realized it was a gift. I thought I should do it for other people, when actually, it was a gift of God to me. As soon as I reflected on that, I felt such peace inside.

Yeshua: Notice the form of that story from the Bible—it came through an interaction with a woman. It was about "knowledge." If you know the Bible, you know that "knowledge" is often a reference to sexuality. The story refers to the flowing water, which stands for the emotions and the heart. This is the Feminine.

There are so many ways these stories can be understood, depending on your consciousness and what resonates for you. I would say the path of opening to the Feminine is a great path of joy and peace. I highly recommend it!

Tom: I long for that peace and joy.

Yeshua: As you should. But it will not come through your thinking mind.

I'm sensing we've touched a deep place. I wish to rest in this place with you for a brief time. Then I think this will be a good ending place for now. Are you at peace with that?

Tom: Yes. I have to stay with being in my heart rather than my head.

Yeshua: You can choose to do that. I recommend it. But it's your choice.

Tom: I want to make that choice, but my head gets in the way.

Yeshua: [laughs] Yes. Your head needs reassurance. This is the work that Mary has so masterfully brought forth. There are emotions that are supporting your choice to go into your head—probably fear. Once you've identified the emotions, you have a choice. Do you simply go into your head and defend yourself from this fear, or do you open to the Feminine? Mary has shown the process of opening to the Feminine that leads to the joy and peace you long for.

Tom: Is that what Mercedes refers to as the "Magdalene Heart Path"?[19]

Yeshua: Yes. Mary's path is part of this great shift out of the third dimension. It's not easy for people to understand. Even now as I say the words "open to the fear," I'm aware that most will not understand the true meaning of that. It's the first step in a deeper process that must be practiced, experienced, and realized. But there is a way through. It's the way of the Feminine.

When you go into your mind to understand something, solve it, and fix it, those are all part of the survival pattern based in fear. When you open yourself to the Feminine, you're making a different choice, inviting a different pathway into your life to follow. This is what will make the difference for most people at this time in terms of growth and evolution and opening up to the next stage of spiritual development. How wonderful that it's such a beautiful process you're being asked to follow. Yet for most, it's very scary.

To let go of the power of the mind—separated from the body, emotions, energy, and sexuality—and open to what is beneath the mind [laughs gently]. That is terrifying for most people. But this is the heart of what will support you in your growth. To do so requires letting go of allegiance to beliefs that support living in the mind, staving off fear, and instead opening to the Feminine in a very different way.

Has this been helpful for you?

Tom: Yes, very much. I need to sit with it and allow it to come from within rather than trying to figure it out.

Yeshua: Wonderful. We shall continue at another time when it feels right to do so.

Tom: Yes, we will do that. I have tons of questions [laughs].

Yeshua: And I have tons of answers [laughs heartily]. Infinite, in fact [laughs again]. Perhaps it would be better to say I have tons of responses. I support you in finding the answers that your soul is calling for at this moment and which I believe many others are calling for as well.

Tom: Thank you so much for today. I really appreciate it.

Yeshua: Blessings to you, beloved brother.

Tom: Blessings to you and to Mary Magdalene too.

FOUR

Fear of the Feminine

Yeshua: Blessings, dear one. This is Yeshua. I've returned, and I'm happy to resume our conversation. My desire is to begin with you, Tom, to see what you wish to continue or to explore at this time.

Tom: Thank you for this time together, Yeshua. Thank you for being so welcoming, loving, open, and freeing. Being with you makes my heart feel good.

After listening to the recording of our last conversation, I realized I was stuck in my agenda and in the Masculine. I felt I had to get through my questions in a hurry so as not to waste your time. It was almost embarrassing. You gave me so many opportunities to rise above my tunnel vision, to ask questions, and to delve further into what you were saying, but I kept bulldozing along, even cutting you off. I was in my head, not my heart. I'm sorry. I'm not good at thinking on the spot.

I'd like to revisit something from our last conversation. You spoke about third-dimensional consciousness as rooted in power structures and authority over others. The belief that we're disconnected from the divine results in fear. For many of us, the ultimate fear is death, which we believe will end it all. Consequently, we long for some ultimate power that will save us from whatever is going to get us.

As I reflect on what you said, I sense that understanding this third-dimensional experience is the key to moving forward. It impacts all we do. Otherwise, all that follows will be incomplete and superficial. So, my first question is this: how did the third-dimensional consciousness of power structures and authority over others begin?

Yeshua: First, I wish to say that your understanding is very accurate. You are, from my perspective, in a deep process of self-understanding and self-liberation. I thank you for giving voice to this. It gives me hope that your voice can help others awaken to these same understandings.

I want to go back to what you first communicated today. In reflecting on our previous session, you said you were embarrassed. I also imagine you feel some regret. These feelings are because you were sticking to an agenda rather than being fully present with what was happening. Is my understanding accurate?

Tom: Yes, it's very accurate. I felt I needed to get through my questions, so I wasn't letting our interaction flow by itself. I was trying to control it.

Yeshua: Yes. Why do you think you were doing that?

Tom: I have difficulty thinking on the spur of the moment, for one thing.

Yeshua: If you're not able to think on the spur of the moment, what are you afraid might happen?

Tom: I'm afraid I'll get off track or go in the wrong direction or something. I guess maybe it's the fear of doing something wrong.

Yeshua: Exactly. So, if you aren't able to stay on track with your mind, you're left with fear.

Tom: Yes.

Yeshua: And that is the great fear. Do you understand?

Tom: Could you say that again please?

Yeshua: You've gotten in touch with the fact that sticking to your agenda rather than letting go is a form of power and control. You're also in touch with what is beneath that control, which is fear.

When I asked what would happen if you let go of your control mechanism of sticking to your agenda, your response was that you'd get off track. You wouldn't be able to think clearly in the moment and might go the wrong direction. Then I said, "OK. If you lost your ability to be present and think in the moment, what would be left?" We agreed you'd be left with the fear. That is what you're most afraid of, being in the fear. Does that resonate for you?

Tom: Yes.

Yeshua: Most people have very little experience of allowing themselves to go into their fear. They've been so well trained to cover their fear with their mind that they don't know what it would be like to set their mind aside and be with the fear.

Tom: I feel it would be a total liberation. [Tom and Yeshua laugh.]

Yeshua: That shows you're advanced in the path. Most people assume it would be annihilation. If you're honest, you probably can recognize that you've operated from the more common assumption for most of your life.

Tom: Yes.

Yeshua: Otherwise, why would you be running from the fear? Why would you always be covering it over with your mind?

Perhaps now you're opening to other ideas, other ways of relating that suggest it wouldn't be annihilation to open to the fear—that it would actually be, as you're saying, liberation. But that's probably not yet the base-level place you're coming from because your actions are still trying to avoid the fear.

Tom: Yes.

Yeshua: Perhaps communicating with me brings up fear more than in other circumstances where you feel safer, more relaxed, or have more trust. Perhaps with me there are triggers that go off for you about my being an authority, someone with great power. Perhaps that was the way you related to me when you were part of the Catholic Church. I'm guessing that may be a part of it too. Do you think that's accurate?

Tom: Yes. Yet in the midst of that, just listening to you seems so freeing. You take everything I say and don't argue with me [laughs].

Yeshua: Why should I argue? I'm not threatened by it. One only argues when one is threatened.

Tom: You're so free. I wish I could be that way.

Yeshua: You're underway. You're well on your path. And I hope my communication will support that further.

Tom: Yes.

Yeshua: Let's go to this fear of what happens if the mind dissolves, doesn't function, and doesn't protect you. Then you're left with only the fear. Can you contact it?

Tom: A picture of my childhood comes up.

Yeshua: What picture is that?

Tom: I was at a birthday party, and we were swimming. There must have been a cliff and a deep part at the bottom. Suddenly, I stepped off the ledge, and there was nothing to hold onto. I was grasping and yelling for help, but everyone was having too much fun, and they didn't hear me.

 Then a wave came and pushed me back onto the solid part, and I was OK! Later I thanked God for bringing that wave that moved me to safety.

Yeshua: Someone heard you very clearly!

Tom: Yes, someone did [laughs]. But I had nothing to grasp onto. It was a real vulnerability.

Yeshua: Real vulnerability. Yes. Do you see that this is the position of human beings in embodiment? You realize you can lose your embodiment and survival at any moment. With the awareness of embodiment comes the awareness of death and loss, perhaps not in a conscious way but in a primal way. Even infants feel it. When an infant falls, there's a primal fear, *Will I be caught?* They don't know what it is; they just know the primal fear. You can hear it in their cry.

As soon as you're born into embodiment and become conscious, you become conscious of your vulnerability. It's survival vulnerability, vulnerability to death. As soon as you're conscious of life, you're conscious of death. *All* of that is the Feminine. All of form is the Feminine.

This isn't gender; it's the archetypal Feminine. This isn't even about human beings as women or girls. This is the archetypal Feminine that all humans have. You can call it yin-yang; it's the same thing. You can give it any name or label. But calling it "Feminine" is valuable because it does have a relationship with women. I will get back to that.

The Pure Masculine

Yeshua: Before human beings came into embodiment, you were in what I would call the pure Masculine—which is formless, infinite, and eternal with no beginning or end. It's the transcendental divine being. In that state there's no form or embodiment, so there's no loss of that. There's no death. This is what the pure Masculine in all of you seeks.

All of you are this pure, divine being. In general, Eastern religions have tended to focus on this aspect. That's why meditation is such an intrinsic part of Eastern religions because meditation connects you with this transcendental part of yourself, that which is beyond and prior to manifestation.

Do you have a sense of what I'm talking about? Have you ever had the experience of this absolutely free part of yourself that's eternal and infinite?

Tom: I can think of certain situations where I've had an experience, and I wanted to weep. I've been in the mountains, and I just wanted to cry. I'm not sure if that's what you're referring to or not.

Yeshua: I'm not sure either. I imagine what you're describing is different because the Masculine is associated with peace and liberation. Are you a meditator?

Tom: I do meditate. But as I listen to you, I think I probably meditate more with my head. I try to get to my heart, and finally I say, "I'm not going to have any ideas. I'm just going to be there." I keep telling my wife I don't seem to be getting anywhere. [Tom and Yeshua chuckle.]

Yeshua: Have you ever had a sense of being lifted beyond yourself into some pure state? You're not totally disconnected; you could reconnect with yourself in your ordinary way at any time. You still have that choice. But you have a sense of being in something greater.

Tom: I'm thinking about the time I was on retreat, and suddenly I felt stopped by some mysterious force. I started to weep, and after that, the Scripture passage I'd been struggling with ("We know and we believe the love that God has for us")[20] came alive for me. Finally, nothing stopped me from saying, "We know and we believe." I'm not sure if that's what you're asking. Maybe I haven't experienced what you're describing.

Yeshua: Most people experience this transcendental state in glimpses, especially people who are drawn to spirituality. But they may not recognize what they're experiencing as the transcendental state. In general, those openings greatly motivate people to want to experience the transcendental state more often.

The Feminine Divine

Yeshua: You've been on the path of Christianity, which, like most Western spiritual paths, tends to be more focused on the Feminine. The Feminine is the path of finding God in the midst of form and manifestation. This may happen when an individual sees an exquisite sunset or spends time in the mountains or at the ocean or is somehow connected with nature, and they feel their heart open. You described that you often weep. That's generally a response to being touched by the Feminine divine. It's feeling God, however you relate to God, communicated through form and manifestation, through the earth, through something in nature.

When parents see their own child being born, they often have an overwhelming feeling of love. That's the Feminine. That's feeling the divine in manifestation, incarnation. The love most parents have for their child, even throughout the child's life, is the pure expression of the Feminine divine.

Tom: Like my wife loving me.

Yeshua: Yes, that's another form. It's why, in your world, there's such an incredible drive for relationship and union with a partner.

That's one of the most powerful ways human beings experience the Feminine divine—as love.

Yet without the partnering of the Masculine divine—the pure consciousness, the freedom, the state of already being liberated— the Feminine, in and of itself, isn't sufficient. You see, the Feminine is the essence of change. The Feminine is always changing. Your partner is always changing, your children are always changing, the weather is always changing, and Earth is always changing.

The Feminine manifests as the cycle of birth, life, death, and rebirth. This can be an entire lifecycle, such as human beings go through in their lifetimes. But the cycle also occurs in every moment. When you get an idea, you're giving birth. When you carry it out, there's life. When you let go of it, there's death. When it comes in a new form, it's rebirth. Every moment can be seen as the Feminine cycle.

In contrast, the Masculine *never* changes. Eternity does not change. Infinity does not change. Some of your Eastern religions, such as Buddhism, refer to this, calling it the *pure land*—pure because it's not involved with all the changes of manifestation.

The Eastern and Western Paths

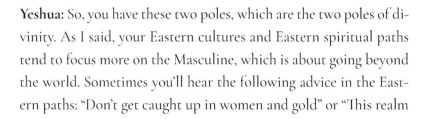

Yeshua: So, you have these two poles, which are the two poles of divinity. As I said, your Eastern cultures and Eastern spiritual paths tend to focus more on the Masculine, which is about going beyond the world. Sometimes you'll hear the following advice in the Eastern paths: "Don't get caught up in women and gold" or "This realm is suffering." They call this realm *maya*, which means illusion. These are tools to help people discover what's beyond this realm, that which never changes.

When I spoke of God the Father, that was the best I could come up with to speak to the culture and consciousness of the people at that time because they were very connected to the Feminine. They were very Earth-based and dependent on nature in a way your modern world isn't. Your modern world has become dissociated from the Feminine, from nature in particular, but really from the Feminine in all aspects. There are many reasons for this. Your technology has been very influential in dissociating your modern world from the Feminine and physical manifestation.

Two thousand years ago, people were deeply connected to the Feminine, and for the most part they were not very connected to the pure Masculine. Even their understanding of God was as a being with form, an old man with a beard sitting on a throne. He was more like a king than God. I made use of this metaphor of Father to help people grow stronger in their connection to this aspect of divinity, the Masculine aspect.

But my partner and my beloved, Mary Magdalene, was also being, demonstrating, and teaching about the Feminine, which is ultimately about *love*. Yet the world wasn't ready. People were much too fearful, and their relationship with women was already one of power and domination. This wasn't just in relation to women. It was in relation to the Feminine altogether. But it certainly included women. It was the beginning of what is often called the patriarchy.

It wasn't time, so what was recorded was only half. It was the part about God the Father.

The Feminine is incarnation in form. The Feminine is what all of you are. When the Feminine got cut out, you cut yourself out. You cut out your body, your sexuality, and your emotions. And you cut women in embodiment out. You've lost huge parts of yourself, huge parts of your reality. The great loss in all of this is that the Feminine is what you came here to know and experience. You incarnated here to find your way to God through knowing and experiencing the Feminine.

Where you came from was the place of the pure Masculine. You didn't need to come here to know the Masculine. You were already connected to the Masculine prior to coming here—perhaps not completely but certainly far more than you are now.

Ultimately, before this whole realm of Earth and 3-D came into being, prior to all that, you were simply in the Masculine. And as the Masculine you longed for more. This is the meaning of Adam and Eve. Adam was longing for more. Adam was lonely. It's a story. You don't need to take it literally. It certainly has nothing to do with proving how human beings are sinful or damned in any way. That's a total misunderstanding. It's a story pointing to the original place that humans came from and still know within themselves. Perhaps not consciously but at some level of your being you know that place of freedom and purity, and part of you longs for that transcendent reality.

Another part of you longs to know God in the midst of this manifest world. That part of you, generally, is afraid because, as creation goes, you're new to that part. Human beings are new to manifesting in this Feminine form of birth, life, and death. You don't have your "sea legs" yet. You don't know how to find God in this. And you especially don't know how to stay connected to the wholeness of the prior Masculine God while relating to the Feminine God.

Do you understand? Are you with me?

Tom: Yes. I do experience that longing. I'm not even sure what that longing is, but it's there.

Yeshua: Yes. Yes.

Human beings have created two great paths, the Eastern path and the Western path. The Eastern path says, "Forget this place. We need to get out of here. We need to go back to that prior transcendence, that pure place. This place is suffering. We need to get out of suffering to the place that's pure, where we're free—free of suffering and all limitations." The Eastern path is right and true, but it's only half of the picture.

The Western path says, "We must find God here." At the earliest stages, it's about simply surviving. But once survival feels sufficiently secure, then it's about knowing greater aspects of divinity in this realm. Power is one of those aspects.

Becoming the Lover

Yeshua: Power, the power to create, is an aspect of God. God has ultimate power. In this Earth realm, power is one of the great arenas and platforms that's being experienced, understood, and hopefully grown with. But it's taking a great deal of time because it's one of the major lessons, and many people have become distracted. Then they think things such as, *Perhaps power is its own god that will save us.*

Tom: Yes.

Yeshua: Many people hope to find God through power, as opposed to finding God and finding God's power. It's a false god that many people seek. It's the god of separation. This is a great lesson for many at this time. It's a yearning for God. But it's being expressed as, *Perhaps the god of power will be the god that will save us from the great fear of annihilation.*

Tom: That's why we have all these wars.

Yeshua: That's the *why* of almost *everything* that human beings do. You want to get ahead in your work and have power in your re-lationships. The striving for power informs and affects so many arenas until you realize it's taking you away from the true God. Seeking power in those ways does not bring fulfillment. It doesn't bring you joy or freedom. It takes spiritual maturity to realize this.

If you let go of that striving for power, what are you left with? Fear. Sooner or later, you're left with the Feminine. Chasing after power is part of the Masculine, but in a lower form than the pure Masculine. It's a more ordinary form.

The Feminine, in its more ordinary and practical form, is about surrender, acceptance, openness, and receiving rather than asser-tion and accomplishment. So, the Feminine path is very different. It's good to be full and mature in both—to have access to the Femi-nine and the Masculine and to be united in both within you. Your world has spent a long time developing the Masculine side while dealing with the Feminine [laughs].

Most of you are familiar with the more practical Masculine, as opposed to the higher or exalted pure Masculine. You call it masculinity—being assertive or even aggressive, goal-oriented, and accomplishing things.

Tom: The warrior.

Yeshua: Yes, the warrior. And the magician. The magician is about the power of the mind. Both are about power. The warrior uses physical power. The magician uses mental power. Together they make up the practical side of the Masculine in embodiment. But there's another side to the Masculine: the lover. The lover opens to the Feminine. Humanity is on the cusp of opening to the Feminine, which goes beyond the fear of annihilation and destruction, beyond the fear of fear itself.

In your world, many men are scared to open to women or even to acknowledge their fear of opening to women.

What does opening to the Feminine look like? It looks like opening to emotions. It looks like listening to women and trusting them rather than arguing and discounting them. It looks like opening to the Feminine form of sexuality, which is not about domination but union. This is the great moment you're in.

How often have your church authorities stood up for the Feminine in these forms?

Tom: They haven't stood up much for the Feminine.

Yeshua: That is true.

Tom: In fact, they've controlled the Feminine over the ages. Women who felt called to do certain things were often put down, rejected, and denied.

Yeshua: Killed. Look at the great controversy over the idea that I was a sexual being.

Tom: Yes.

Yeshua: That's taboo because it would suggest that I was open to the Feminine. To cut out the Feminine, it was necessary to make me asexual and to make my mother asexual.

Tom: And that's why priests have to be celibate.

Yeshua: Supposedly. [Yeshua and Tom laugh.] It was necessary to cut out that I had any lover and deny that Mary Magdalene ever existed as my lover. She was only allowed to be someone who was dominated by me. It had to be clear, and then she could be marginally included, though relegated to probably being a whore.

Tom: That's right.

Yeshua: It was a very methodical program to eliminate the Feminine.

Tom: When I heard you were married, I was so excited and happy.

Yeshua: Why would I not be married? What does it say about marriage and about women to assume that, if I'm God, I would not be married? What is that message? What is the message if there is only God the Father and not God the Mother? What are all these messages saying? That only the Masculine is holy. This is the message of fear of the Feminine.

    The great turning point is to set that domination aside. The beginning is to look at the fear and then go beyond it, not by denying it but by opening to it. This is the beginning of becoming the lover.

Your expression at the beginning of our time together today— when you expressed your embarrassment and regret about staying in your mind, and you connected to the fear that was beneath those thoughts—that was you opening to the lover.

This is not just love of the Feminine. This is love of God. All of manifestation is the Feminine divine. If you cut that out from God, you're at war with yourself, and you're at war with everything else.

You're beginning to lift the curtain, the veil of all the indoctrination that says only the Masculine is holy. You're beginning to open to an entirely different reality, to an entirely different life, an entirely different understanding. That new understanding says, *This was just one version, one way the story could be penned. But I don't like that version. I don't like being at war with myself and reality—or at least half of reality. But it's the prominent half, the half I deal with throughout my life.* Look at the stress of fighting incarnation for a lifetime.

This is the amazing gift that Mary Magdalene, as the representative of the Divine Feminine, the Feminine God, brings. Mary says humanity's path is about loving the body, including the body of Earth. It's about loving sexuality. It's about loving emotions, both painful and pleasurable. And it's about being skilled in all these forms of loving, especially with regard to emotions.

Skills and wisdom are available for making emotions your greatest ally to connect you with God *most directly*. Emotions connect you first with the Feminine God, but the great secret of the Feminine God is that she's *in love* with the Masculine God. She always brings you to the Masculine. The pathway of the Feminine God is incredibly direct. Not only that, it's what you came here to learn. And now Mary is sharing this with people.

Emotions aren't the only pathway. Your sexuality is also a pathway to God but not in the way most of you practice it. Most of you practice sexuality out of fear, domination, and power. But that's not the only possibility. Mary describes skills for relating to sexuality in a way that connects you to God. Similarly, there are skills of being embodied and relating to the body, such that embodiment and form connect you to God.

But of these three—the body, sexuality, and emotions—Mary says the greatest work most human beings have to do at this time relates to emotions. This is partly because human beings have a purpose in the bigger picture. At the cosmic level, human beings were intended to be leaders in the emotional realm.

You've shied away from this role for the most part and are quite underdeveloped in your strength and leadership in this arena. Instead of opening to your fear, you've learned to run away to your mind and dominate it. This is the way the Masculine has dominated the Feminine—through the mind.

The Feminine is not out to kill your mind. The Feminine is out to unite with your mind, to make you whole. But you must become the warrior of the Masculine and stand up to your fear. You must become the great magician of the Masculine and learn the skills of opening to the Feminine. Then you will be worthy and prepared to be a lover.

I have said a great deal.

Tom: You certainly have. My understanding is that I've incarnated many times to work on this. I hope I'm finally getting it, that I'm finally addressing and facing my fears. I keep speaking in Masculine terms, but I want to open myself to what's underneath and move beyond the fear.

Yeshua: Yes. You've already taken great steps in this direction by standing up to an enormous institution, which also included standing up to your family and to your beliefs, which were instilled from a young age. You turned instead to a woman who's become a great part of your spiritual guidance and support. Is that right?

Tom: I call her my ascended master. [Yeshua and Tom chuckle.]

Yeshua: Yes.

Tom: I am so, so fortunate to have her.

Yeshua: If you want to support the process more, begin to study the Feminine path, just as women have studied the Masculine path. Women have developed their minds. They've developed their ability to accomplish, to be warriors when needed, to be magicians and figure things out. Women have done this, but men are behind. If you want to accelerate your spiritual process, begin to study. Apply the strength of your magician to learn. Use the strength of your warrior to apply yourself to the Feminine path. Through this you'll accelerate your process of opening to the Feminine immensely.

Tom: We both have read *Mary Magdalene Beckons*. Ann wants to go through it together, but I have been a little hesitant. I want to do it with her though.

Yeshua: Yes. And make use of the Magdalene Heart Path course.[21] Few men have stepped up to that so far. The ones who have are the warriors and magicians. These are the ones who are strong enough to open themselves to the next phase of becoming the lover. They bring their strength as warriors and magicians into the realm of the lover.

This is human evolution at play. It's the great turning point for humanity. And it's happening, mostly led by the Feminine. To become a great leader, a great hero, a great king of the Masculine, it's necessary to move into this next arena of the lover.

Tom: We keep hearing that now is a time like never before. Transformation is happening. We're praying for this and want to raise our vibration for this. What you're saying is that we need to accept the Feminine to move forward.

Yeshua: Absolutely. It's not to deny the Masculine. It's to bring the strength of the Masculine, to open to the Masculine as the *lover* of the Feminine—lover of the body, sexuality, emotions, Earth, and women. Lover. This is the next great horizon. This is why I taught about love. But I didn't do it in isolation. I did it with *my* lover: my Feminine Goddess incarnate.

Tom: It's so sad that Mary was deleted from the story.

Yeshua: It is only temporary. They could never completely abolish or annihilate her. She's actually growing exponentially in people's awareness and in their hearts. It was simply a seed that needed a lot of time to germinate.

Tom: I'm so happy about that.

Yeshua: [chuckles] It's the savior of your species; I assure you. [Yeshua laughs along with Tom.]

Tom: This has been wonderful, Yeshua.

Yeshua: Perhaps this is a good resting place for today.

Tom: Yes. However, I want to refer back to the end of our last conversation when you said, "I'm sensing in this moment that we're in a very deep place. I wish to rest in this place with you for a brief time." But I kept on talking and talking. I never made the choice to be still, and I regret that. I wanted to be still with you, but I kept on talking.

Yeshua: Because if you're still, the first thing you'll confront is your fear.

Tom: Yet I want to be one with you. You gave me the chance, but I kept talking.

Yeshua: Because the fear was there. How is the fear right now?

Tom: It's much less. I feel so good with all you've said.

Yeshua: Yes. This was the great healing work I came to do. The healing work I did of the physical is what was recorded because it's what people could understand. But it's not the true healing. The true healing heals all that separates you from God.

Loving the physical is wonderful, and healing the physical is a form of loving it. But even bigger than that is to love the emotions and heal the fear of the emotions. This will heal a great deal of your separation from God. So, make use of Mary's teaching.

Tom: OK.

Yeshua: Her teaching helps take the fear out of the emotions, replacing fear with wisdom and the understanding that emotions are a gift. They're guidance to help you connect to God in the way you long for. Make use of them.

Tom: Thank you for that.

Yeshua: You're welcome, my beloved brother. Thank you for who you are. Thank you for the voice you are willing to be. You're a great voice of humanity's longing and courage. It took courage to become a priest, to step out of the normal worldly path and take on such an aspiration and discipline. And it took courage to step out of that—this time standing up to another structure of authority, the Church itself. It took courage to question the beliefs you were told ought never to be questioned. It takes courage to dialogue with me. I thank you for your courage.

Tom: Thank you for being so loving to me.

Yeshua: It is my great joy to be loving. That's the embrace of the Feminine divine. You're on your path to know this great joy as well. I'm sure you already do. And you can know it even more.

Tom: Yes. Thank you.

Yeshua: Blessings, my dear, dear brother. I look forward to more. I'm so happy to dialogue with you.

Tom: Thank you. And say hi to Mary Magdalene.

Yeshua: I certainly will.

FIVE

You Chose to Be Here

Yeshua: Hello, dear one. This is Yeshua. I return and am happy to join you once again. Let us move right into your questions and material for today. What would you like to begin with?

Tom: Hello, Yeshua. Thank you so much for coming back. What a powerful and wonderful experience our last session was for me, particularly your explanation about the Masculine and Feminine. It almost boggles the mind how much was in there. Thank you for clarifying so many things. Yet there are many things I have questions about.

First, I'd like to speak about creating our reality. I have difficulty understanding this. How do I create my reality? What does that mean?

Yeshua: You are already creating your reality. You might want to learn how to do it more consciously. Everything you do creates your reality. Everything you are creates your reality.

In the third dimension, you're operating somewhat like a machine. Every moment of choice programs the machine for what the machine is going to bring back to you. So, every choice you make is ultimately creating your reality. This is not just in the third dimension. This is in all dimensions. However, in the third dimension it has a more mechanical quality [laughs] You are less conscious, less aware of what's happening.

Also, in the third dimension it takes more effort to make things happen. If you have something you want to accomplish—let's say you want to remove a tree from your yard—that takes effort, right?

Tom: Yes.

Yeshua: In the fourth dimension—which is more like what you experience in your dreams—if you want to remove the tree from your front yard, you think the thought, and boom, it's gone. Right?

Tom: That's right.

Yeshua: Not so much effort. Much easier. In the third dimension it takes effort to manifest, but you're always manifesting. Even your thoughts are manifesting. However, if you're not putting effort into following up, the manifestation will tend to take a great deal of time and not be as productive. Nonetheless, everything you're doing is creating your reality.

Have you ever had a friend who you shared certain parts of your reality with—maybe you worked together or belonged to the same church, or you're neighbors—but their experience was so different from yours? At work they may have been getting into fights while you found your associates very compatible. Or maybe their house got broken into but yours didn't. Or perhaps they were having a more wonderful experience than you were. Everything seemed to come easily to them. Why is that? Why do people in the same situation have different experiences? Do you think it's just random?

Tom: It's probably creation. [Tom and Yeshua laugh.]

Yeshua: Yes. And it's not just from this life. It's from previous lives too. This is what's called karma, which involves experiencing your creations from previous lifetimes too. In the third dimension, people sometimes view karma as punishment and reward. They think you're being punished for bad things you did in the past and rewarded for good things. This is a great limitation. This is part of third-dimensional consciousness.

When you go beyond the third dimension, you go beyond the whole notion of good and bad, right and wrong. From my perspective, karma has nothing to do with good or bad and punishments or rewards. It has to do with learning what your soul came to grow in and learn about. If you're not complete with that particular learning, then it still affects you. When you're complete, you become free of it, and it no longer limits you. Then you move into a freedom of manifestation and conscious creation rather than creating out of past choices, habits, or unconscious programming.

Ultimately, it's all choice because your soul has chosen to be here. Before this lifetime, your soul chose the circumstances you would have here to support the kind of growth and experiences your soul is longing for.

This is a free-choice realm. In the third dimension, you don't tend to understand or be aware of that. It's part of what could be called "the veil" that covers your awareness, your consciousness. You think things are just happening to you as opposed to realizing, *I'm creating this.*

You could call this victim consciousness. It's quite an epidemic in the third dimension [laughs]. People believe everything is just happening to them, and they have nothing to do with it [more laughter].

It's quite a shift in your spiritual evolution when you start to realize, *I'm choosing this. I'm responsible for this.* There's a stage as you first move into this understanding where this might feel like a burden or difficult, challenging. At this stage you may think, *I'm at fault for all this.* That thinking comes from a third-dimensional consciousness. If you're able to move beyond that, you can see that it's tremendously empowering to assume responsibility for what's happening. Now you have a choice. You can choose something else. If you're simply the recipient, the victim of circumstances that are being placed upon you, you're powerless.

Tom: I keep forgetting how powerful I am.

Yeshua: Yes. There are a great many things that you'll start to remember as you awaken.

Tom: Yes. I'm thinking about a friend whose four-year-old granddaughter has suffered with leukemia nearly all her life. She has gone through so much in her short life. I've wondered, *How can this be?* I keep forgetting there's choice happening here. I have no control over it.

Yeshua: No, you have tremendous control over it.

Tom: Not her choice.

Yeshua: Not her choice but your choice. Imagine how differently you and everyone else would relate to this child if you related to her as having chosen this. I'm not suggesting an unconscious, separating, closed position, such as, *Tough luck! You chose it; suffer the consequences!* What I'm suggesting is very different, where you understand her choice as sacred.

This is not to deny the difficulty and pain of her choice—the physical pain, the emotional pain for herself, her family, her loved ones. That, too, was part of her choice. Imagine how differently you might relate through honoring that choice.

Tom: I need to free myself of something to be able to see it that way. That's what you would call God's perspective. Is that right?

Yeshua: Absolutely.

Tom: I have to really expand my vision to see it.

Yeshua: What is blocking that expansion? Is it the belief that this is a cruel thing?

Tom: I guess I'm wondering why somebody would choose all that pain.

Yeshua: Very good question. What benefit might the soul receive from choosing such pain?

Tom: Compassion for oneself?

Yeshua: Possibly.

Tom: Some learning here.

Yeshua: Yes. Souls often incarnate in a number of lives—often a series of lives—where they're exploring a particular aspect of being. Perhaps this soul is exploring physical pain or physical limitation. Perhaps the soul is exploring powerlessness. There could be all sorts of things. You wouldn't really know unless you were able to know that soul's path. But they're working on something through this manifestation.

The other thing souls sometimes do is agree to certain circumstances in support of other beings. Perhaps they're supporting the family in an experience the family is working on. There can be various reasons, and often there is more than one reason. Often the soul itself is working on something that having that condition will support, and it will also support the family members in other ways. The way our souls choose to work together in lifetimes is quite an amazing puzzle.

Tom: Is this similar to the idea that Source wants to experience manifestation in form?

Yeshua: Absolutely.

Tom: So we're helping Source experience all these different elements?

Yeshua: We're not helping Source experience it. We *are* Source experiencing itself [laughs].

Tom: I guess we have to be open to that because Source is open to all of this.

Yeshua: You don't have to be open to it, but it would be to your benefit.

Tom: Yes, yes.

Yeshua: You can choose that freely too.

You Are the Feminine

Tom: With regard to being open, I guess I'm thinking of horrendous things that I'm judgmental about.

Yeshua: Yes, like murder and rape.

Tom: Yes. How am I to be nonjudgmental about that?

Yeshua: That is your choice. Do you want to be judgmental? [laughs] Do you enjoy being judgmental?

Tom: Well, I must enjoy it because I'm judgmental a lot.

Yeshua: What's the alternative to being judgmental? Being judgmental is simply a protection. What are you protecting yourself from by being judgmental?

Tom: I suppose the pain that might be happening.

Yeshua: Yes, yes.

Tom: So I send love and light.

Yeshua: You can't send love and light when you're completely suppressing yourself.

Tom: Pardon me? I can't send love and light?

Yeshua: [laughs] No. All you can send is your own contraction [laughs again]. You send your fear.

Tom: What's the middle step then? What do I do?

Yeshua: You choose not to go into the defenses of the mind and instead stay in experience. Have the full experience. This is the Masculine allowing itself to descend fully into the realm of the Feminine. This is the great terror for the Masculine.

Tom: Hmm . . . to go fully into it.

Yeshua: You're ultimately going fully into yourself. You already are fully into it. You're just running away at the speed of light—at the speed of mind, you might say. Yet this is what you came here for.

Tom: Yes, you mentioned that last time. We came to experience the Feminine, the manifestation.

Yeshua: Yes. And you love certain parts of the Feminine, I'm sure.

Tom: Yes.

Yeshua: You love the beauty, sensuality, sexuality, joy, love, and connection. Yet the Feminine is not only that. The Feminine is also death, destruction, and pain. You cannot cut off from one without cutting off from the other. Your world has been largely created to cut off the Feminine because of not wanting to experience the parts of the Feminine that most people are terrified of: death, destruction, and pain.

In your fear you believe that to open to these aspects of the Feminine will harm you. Those beliefs are not accurate. They come from the Masculine fear of the Feminine. The truth is, what harms you is holding off from the Feminine. It harms the Feminine as well.

Tom: I just felt a little teary as I heard that, that I've got to allow myself to be me.

Yeshua: Yes because you are the Feminine. You are fully embodied. You have your feelings, your sexuality, and your energy. You're not only the Feminine; you're also the Masculine. But cutting off from the Feminine is cutting off from yourself.

In your world, this is what happens for boys, especially. They're told that the Feminine part of themselves cannot be included, that they won't be loved and rewarded if they exhibit the Feminine parts of themselves. For boys this prohibition is especially strong around showing any emotion other than anger and aggression or showing any other Feminine traits. It's communicated clearly in many, many ways that such expressions are taboo, and people will be ostracized if they make such choices. So, men, especially, are suffering from the taboo against the Feminine.

Tom: It all centers on fear and being open to fear.

Yeshua: Yes. The fear of the Feminine, the fear of fully coming here, fully allowing.

This hasn't always been the case in your world, and there are still places where this fear is much less predominant. The places you call indigenous cultures are much more accepting of the Feminine. Even some of your developed cultures are more accepting of emotions, the body, and sexuality. But many of your developed cultures restrict these parts of yourself. The result has been a recourse to living from the mind, with extreme distance, separation, and disconnection from your bodies, sexuality, emotions, and the physical world. You're seeing the consequences of this refusal of the Feminine in your world.

Tom: In an earlier conversation, you talked about humanity being one of the leaders, showing the rest of the universe about emotions. Are we to be teachers of the universe?

Yeshua: Leaders in that you are the models of emotions. You are the demonstrators.

Tom: Do beings in other worlds have emotions like we do, or are we unique?

Yeshua: All beings are unique. The depth and breadth of human emotions is a particular aspect of human beings' uniqueness.

What is going on for you right now?

Tom: My task now—or our task—is to move into and become open to emotions.

Yeshua: Absolutely. And then to learn the process whereby emotions take you into God-connection. This is what my beloved Mary Magdalene has been showing and guiding people in: the Feminine path, which is virtually unknown, especially in your spiritual worlds. Yet it's a direct path for full God connection and communion, much more so than the rite of drinking some sips of wine and eating some wafers backed up by centuries of thinking and belief [laughs].

Free Yourself from Mental Slavery

Tom: I was going to bring that up today.

Yeshua: [laughs] Go for it.

Tom: This is something I was brought up with, the so-called Last Supper. "Take this bread, this is my body; take this wine, this is my blood." I think to myself, *The Church said this is Jesus's real body and blood, but they said it's an un-bloody sacrifice.*

Yeshua: [laughs] They've got all the answers, don't they? [more laughter]

Tom: And when they said to eat this, the word they used is "masticate." As a child, we weren't even supposed to allow the wafer to touch our teeth. I thought, *How do I masticate this if I can't allow it to touch my teeth?*

Yeshua: Maybe they made a mistake and they meant "masturbate" [laughs].

Tom: I'm understanding this is not what you did. You might have said, "When you get together to eat you might remember me."

Yeshua: No, no, no, no, no, no, no, no, no, no, no, no, no! This whole thing is based on the idea that you can't be God. Only I am God. Only I am the Son of God. And we're all males. It's a male club, and blah, blah, blah.

This is ridiculous! You have to eat part of my body, so you can have some speck of connection to God? Who came up with that? But you're still very lowly and in sin, right? [laughs]

Tom: Right. We can't receive the Eucharist if we're in sin.

Yeshua: That's right. That's why you need the Church [laughs].

Tom: When there were extra wafers, they would put them (which was you) in the tabernacle. As a child I would wonder, *What does* *it feel like to be in that tabernacle the whole time? It must be like being in prison.*

Yeshua: What makes you think I was there? It's all based on these exceedingly limited ideas of what God is. What if everything is God? What if the bread is the body of God because everything is the body of God?

Tom: I'm not sure about this wafer. It tastes like plastic. [Yeshua laughs.] Anyhow, I shouldn't be negative about it.

Yeshua: No. Instead of being negative, be in your feelings. Your feeling is doubt, doubt that this could possibly be God—this manufactured thing that doesn't taste anything like the aliveness and wonderfulness of the Feminine. Right?

Tom: At the same time, before we received communion, we said, "Lord, I am not worthy to receive you. Lord, I am not worthy to receive you." I think we're worthy because you made us worthy. We're worthy because we're divine.

Yeshua: No, the Lord did not make you worthy [chuckles]. Worthy is a third-dimensional concept. Why would you be here if you weren't worthy? Who's not worthy? What a ridiculous concept! But a brilliant one for controlling people—to determine who's worthy and who's not. Being worthy means you survive, whether it's in this world or the next world. "Sign up here and be my slave, especially my mind slave." Look at the ridiculous ideas you signed up for, just to become worthy. [Yeshua and Tom laugh heartily.]

You have forgotten so much. You have forgotten who you are! You are God. You don't need the Church to redeem you because you're some horrible, slobbering sinner [laughs]. You've forgotten who you are, and you've forgotten how to connect with your highest beingness. And I don't think eating that wafer has done much to help you.

Tom: [chuckles] Initially, the Church said that Jesus came to save us. I'm not even sure what you came to save us from.

Yeshua: Exactly. It's all propaganda. It's all beliefs being propagated to support an institution. Those beliefs, by and large, don't have a lot to do with God. But because so many people think they do, they bring their hearts to this institution, and they find something in it. But it's not because of those beliefs [laughs].

Tom: I suppose for many people just getting together means more than anything else.

Yeshua: Getting together with intention. They have the intention that they're gathering to connect with God. That's a powerful manifestation despite whatever form or belief system it's wrapped up in. You are powerful beings.

Tom: When you said that, I felt a tingling inside, just to remember who we really are. It's almost too much.

Yeshua: It's just enough. Do you want to stop wars? Start feeling. Feeling beings aren't likely to engage in war. Want to stop pedophiles? Start feeling. Feel your own experience until it becomes obvious that everyone else is just like you. Then it becomes unpleasant to hurt another being.

Tom: And we cannot do it for others. Hopefully through feeling, I'm being present to those around me.

Yeshua: Ah, but there's a great secret here.

Tom: OK. What's the secret?

Yeshua: Those who feel, open their hearts. Feeling leads to the heart, and the heart is powerful. It's not powerful in the form of domination. It's powerfully attractive. That's the power of the Feminine, is it not?

Tom: It is.

Yeshua: This is what the Masculine doesn't want you to discover [laughs]. Not only how attractive the Feminine is but how powerful the Feminine is.

Higher-Dimensional Healing

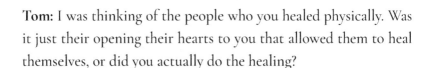

Tom: I was thinking of the people who you healed physically. Was it just their opening their hearts to you that allowed them to heal themselves, or did you actually do the healing?

Yeshua: Healing is a fourth-dimensional capability. It requires both. The people who were healed needed to open and consent to being healed. Then I brought my abilities from the higher dimensions to that healing.

Healing is like your science in some ways. There are principles, techniques, and tools. You have healers in the third dimension who are able to do healing work. You have surgery and medications. Higher-dimensional healing, once you learn it, is similar in the sense that it's an ability. It involves principles and processes, which those who are moved to be healers can learn and engage.

Tom: About four weeks ago, I fell and injured my shoulder. It really hurts. I've been asking all the beings I know to help me to heal. I call on you, the Arcturians—I hear they are healers—Mary Magdalene, and Mother Mary. There's probably a process I need to follow, but I should be able to heal it some way.

Yeshua: First of all, I suggest you surrender your "should." I hear that you would like to be able to heal it. Perhaps it may happen in the way you're hoping. Perhaps that's not your path of healing. Perhaps the healing is going to come in a very different way. Perhaps the healing won't even have the result that you're calling "healing." Perhaps it will be a healing of your emotions, your heart, or your mind. Perhaps it will be a healing of your relationship with life, with God. That may or may not take the physical form of healing you're hoping for.

I recommend and support you in asking for healing. I also recommend you ask for guidance as to what you need to do to support that healing. It's not enough to ask for others to heal you. You must ask what you need to do. And be open to a much greater vision of what healing might look like and the form it might take.

Tom: It means being open to what comes.

Yeshua: Yes. What if you open to the pain of your shoulder? Perhaps you need to ask your shoulder what it wants to communicate to you through this pain. Perhaps you need to open your heart to this pain and your shoulder's experience of it. This is opening to the Feminine.

Tom: Thank you for that. I can't figure it out with my head. It has to be with my heart.

Yeshua: And feeling will guide you there.

Tom: Thank you.

Yeshua: Oftentimes when you're in pain it's because you haven't been listening to your feelings. So, your being has called in a greater feeling, a stronger feeling, to get you to listen. One of your choices is to hear, to open yourself to the pain rather than just try to get rid of it.

Tom: Thank you.

What Happens in Meditation

Tom: You asked me previously if I'm a meditator. I said I meditate every day, but I don't seem to be getting anywhere. I realize meditation is not intended to get me somewhere, but I still feel empty when I'm finished. Could you please say more about meditation and how it might help me or how I can meditate in a better way?

Yeshua: Yes. Often people's first experience of meditation has to do with quieting the body and the mind. This is a good start. Meditation involves temporarily releasing the Feminine. You're releasing all those parts of manifestation—God in manifest form—to open up to the pure Masculine form of God, which you could call "pure consciousness." It has different names in different traditions.

It's also been called "emptiness," "spaciousness," "the witness," "the Self," and "the true self."

The function of meditation is to connect with the pure Masculine, which is a great refreshment from the challenge, even the exhaustion, that can come from being involved in embodiment. Embodiment is not easy all the time. It has many challenges. Meditation is like stepping back from embodiment. You are refreshing and rejuvenating yourself in a bath of pure consciousness.

Embodiment is a great commitment. You see this when people are dying. For many people it's not easy to let go of embodiment. This can be for many reasons. It can come from fear of what's going to happen. *If I let go of embodiment, am I going to be snuffed out, and that's the end? I don't want to be snuffed out.* That's a survival kind of fear. Or it can come from fear of the unknown. It can come from a deep psychophysical attachment to embodiment that must be released and from not knowing how to do that. It's a spiritual process to let go of embodiment.

When beings meditate, they're learning the process of deeply releasing the commitment, or you could say the attachment, to embodiment. As most people who meditate know, letting go of this doesn't lead to death. It leads to the pure state that's prior to embodiment, which you could call "consciousness."

For many people it takes years before they begin to experience the state of pure consciousness while meditating. It can also take a significant time during any particular meditation session to reach this state, anywhere from an hour to an hour and a half. Before that point, you will find that you go through different layers of consciousness.

There's often an initial layer that might feel good—kind of like when you're tired and sit down, and suddenly you feel good. Usually, that feeling doesn't last too long but it's an initial relief.

After that the mind gets activated. Suddenly, all the things you're thinking will start to be displayed. It's like looking at the screen of your mind, and all your thoughts are buzzing around. At a certain point you become aware of what's happening. When you notice that, you begin to have glimpses of, and access to, what's prior to that activity in the mind.

This often leads to a place that's very creative. You start to have creative ideas and solutions to things you've been working on; new ideas come to you. You're still in the mind, but it's a deeper aspect of mind.

If you go beyond this phase, you tend to go into a deeper place of struggle. Here you're struggling with something closer to your core, where your being is attached to the world. This phase might be associated with physical discomfort. You might suddenly have all kinds of physical aches and pains that call to your attention. You want to shift, to get up, to stop meditating. Emotional resistance can come up. So can thoughts. But it's a different quality at this stage, almost like a battle. Part of you is getting closer to letting go, and another part of you is saying, "No, no, no, no, no, no, no!" [Yeshua and Tom chuckle.] The practice is to allow, relax, notice, and observe, and the struggle will play itself out.

At a certain point, your experience will be like clouds parting, and you will start to see the sun. It's the sun of consciousness. At earlier stages in your practice of meditation, these openings may only happen for a few moments. As you develop your practice, they last longer and longer.

Also, at the early stages of practicing meditation, this experience itself can be frightening. When beings finally have the opening they've been longing for, suddenly, they want to end the meditation because of its power [laughs]. It's very powerful. To open yourself to that power is a deep level of surrender, which is a practice in itself for most people.

There's a benefit to all this. As you engage in meditation and get stronger, your practice starts to affect the rest of your life when you're not meditating. It starts to change you. You'll become aware of something more, something that's prior to manifestation, something which precedes this lifetime and will last beyond this lifetime. This new awareness will change how you relate to embodiment.

What I've described is the classical Masculine form of meditation. There are also Feminine forms of meditation that are based on following the pathway of emotions or energy, even following the pathway of sexuality. These meditations lead to this same state. They are much less known in your world, but it's time for both to become known. Different beings may choose different paths—the more Masculine path or the more Feminine path—depending on their tendencies, qualities, and what is easier for them. Ultimately, it's valuable to have access to all.

Does that answer your question?

Tom: Yes. Thank you very much, Yeshua. It's about surrendering to what's going on within me rather than trying to figure out what's going to happen next.

Yeshua: [laughs heartily] Absolutely.

The Essential Difference Between the Feminine and the Masculine

Yeshua: Meditation is a profound practice of surrender. The Masculine form of meditation is about surrendering the Feminine into the pure Masculine.

The Feminine path is the full embrace of the Feminine into the pure Masculine. This is another option. It's what Mary Magdalene is teaching.

This is the difference between the Feminine and the Masculine paths. Masculine forms of meditation are done in an entirely Masculine way. They use Masculine means, such as focus and concentration, to reach pure consciousness, which is the Masculine in its exalted form.

By contrast, the path of the Feminine includes the Masculine. It leads to wholeness. It's time in your world to learn the path of the Feminine, which doesn't exclude the Masculine or the Masculine path, if support of the Masculine is what's needed for balance and well-being.

The great turning point for the Masculine is to trust the Feminine. It's to trust that the Feminine will lead to the Masculine rather than excluding the Masculine in the way the Masculine tends to exclude the Feminine. This is the great learning for the Masculine.

Do you understand what I just said?

Tom: Yes. It's just being there rather than trying to figure it out.

Yeshua: No, that's not what I said. Do you remember at the beginning I said the great fear of the Masculine is surrendering to the Feminine?

Tom: Yes.

Yeshua: The reason this is so fearful for the Masculine is because the Masculine is afraid the Feminine is going to do what the Masculine has done. The Masculine has excluded the Feminine, so the Masculine's fear is that if it surrenders to the Feminine, the Feminine will exclude the Masculine. This is a huge lesson for the Masculine, one that is essential and germane to the point of growth for your world altogether.

The Masculine must understand this essential difference between the Feminine and the Masculine. The Feminine always moves toward inclusion. To surrender to the Feminine is to surrender to that which wants to include the Masculine. When the Masculine can come to a place of trust of the Feminine, through this understanding, your world will change enormously. Have I made things clearer?

Tom: Yes. Thank you. Whenever fear shows up, I need to open up to that fear.

Yeshua: Yes. And it would benefit you to have skills for that opening. This is what—

Tom: Mercedes and Mary Magdalene give us.

Yeshua: Yes, so you aren't lost or flailing in the emotional domain without guidance and wisdom.

Tom: Yes. Those skills are something Ann and I both want to acquire.

The Choice of Vegetarianism

Tom: I have another question, but maybe it's inappropriate. It's about being vegetarian.

Yeshua: Alright.

Tom: Ann and I have been vegetarian for a few years for various reasons. We've heard that meat is difficult to digest, and the hormones given to the animals are dangerous. The horrible conditions the animals live in, the fear and energy they experience while being killed, and our desire to relate to them as conscious beings are all reasons why we've chosen to be vegetarian.

But I'm not sure if this is the right path. We try to consume protein from other foods, but it's not always easy. I've lost weight and some muscle during this time. And visiting with other people is sometimes difficult. Yet we want to be vegetarian.

Do you have ideas about vegetarianism? Were you a vegetarian as an Essene (if you were an Essene)? How can you ask us to eat your body and blood if we're supposed to be vegetarians?

Yeshua: I was going to ask you about that [laughs]. Why are you comfortable eating my body but not an animal's body? [Yeshua and Tom laugh.]

This has to do with your relationship to life and death. If you see death as the end, as some horrible event, then you're going to see all forms of death as bad, sinful, something that shouldn't happen, etc. These are all your mind's judgments.

What if the animals have chosen to be here as their God-beingness? What if they've chosen to feed you in this way? What if they've chosen this form in which their deaths should come, so they can move on to their next phase of beingness as their soul is calling? What if eating an animal is a form of communion just as breathing air is communion and living on Earth is communion? What if it's another form of fully embracing the Feminine?

There's also the matter of loving your body. What does your body require? What would be an act of loving your body, so it can function fully in embodiment? Does it require animal foods? Does it not? Do you feel better when you eat animal foods? Do you not? Can you trust your feelings over your thoughts?

Your feelings for the well-being of animals are very real. Your feelings of pain when you hear about the treatment of animals, the way they're raised, and the foods and chemicals they're given, those concerns are all real. If you choose to eat animals, you can make a choice not to eat animals that live in those conditions, if that's possible and available for you.

Each person's path is different. There is no one "should" or "shouldn't" rule. There's no rule that says "Everyone must be vegetarian!" or "Everyone should eat meat!" It's for you to find your own guidance. It's part of embodiment to find that guidance. You'll find it through your body and your emotions. Your body and your emotions will tell you what you need and don't need, what's right for you, much more than some rule book in your mind.

Tom: I've heard that the plants have given themselves to us as nourishment but not that the animals could have done the same.

Yeshua: [chuckles] And who have you heard this from?

Tom: Various sources. Even those supposedly from other realms.

Yeshua: [laughs heartily] Do not blindly trust sources, whether it's the Catholic Church or someone telling you they're the Queen of Sheba or XYZ from planet ABC. What difference does it make? You're God. You don't need to blindly trust any other sources. Your body is God, and your emotions are God. Let those inform you. You don't need to run away from them and look for the great authority who's going to tell you the right way to live, so that you'll be saved. That's not the game here, and it never was.

You came for embodiment. This is why you're here. Be with your soul. Make use of this great opportunity. Become a lover—a lover of yourself and of other beings. Does being vegetarian support you in being a lover of yourself, including your physical being, or does it take you away?

Tom: Gosh. Right now I can't answer whether being vegetarian helps me to love myself or not.

Yeshua: It may take time. You may have been so involved in your mind and beliefs that to go beneath them may take some time.

Tom: Yes, yes. Thank you so much for this. Thank you so much for incarnating two thousand years ago. I really am sorry the world wasn't ready to accept what you were teaching. But I'm glad you came and taught it and that you were open to the Feminine and to Mary Magdalene.

Yeshua: I am in love with the Feminine. I AM the Feminine. I have no need to hate and eliminate the Feminine. Why would I choose that?

Tom: I'm so grateful Mary Magdalene is there with you as your partner and to bring in the Feminine.

Yeshua: May the world be ready to receive her now. I'm sensing this may be a good stopping place for today.

Tom: Yes, Yeshua. Thank you.

Yeshua: Before we end, I must ask: do you see the light?

Tom: I feel an opening to the light. I don't know if I can see it, but I feel it.

Yeshua: The seeing is not necessarily with your physical eyes.

Tom: It feels like a breath of fresh air.

Yeshua: This is the light of consciousness.

Tom: Thank you.

Yeshua: This is the refreshment of which I speak. You know this. You have experienced this before.

Tom: Yes.

Yeshua: Blessings, my dear one. I love you greatly.

Tom: I love you, too, Yeshua. Thank you.

SIX

Can I Trust Myself?

Yeshua: Hello, dear one. This is Yeshua. I'm happy to be with you once again and to be continuing this process, which I hope will be of great value to many. Please let me hear what's on your mind and in your heart as we continue this journey together.

Tom: Thank you very much, Yeshua, for your guidance and wisdom and in particular for your patience with me. I feel like I'm in a cosmic dance of moving two steps forward and one step back. You've not only responded to my questions over the last three conversations. You have gently taken me on an inner journey, guiding me beneath the surface, and explaining how the third-dimensional consciousness operates.

What you've been sharing with me seems so good and true. It makes my heart feel good. My wife, Ann, says she sees a difference in me. Since our last guidance, I've spent time reflecting on our conversations and receiving much more out of them. I feel excited about what I'm finally getting.

I think I haven't realized the depth of what you're saying. You mentioned that not everyone will understand what you're saying. I feel afraid and embarrassed about this. Part of me thinks that perhaps you should be speaking to someone else who can better understand and help others than I can.

You've given me a way forward through opening to the Feminine and particularly through opening to my emotions. However—and you've noticed this more than I have—I keep returning to my mind and my thinking rather than going below the surface. I seem to be hanging on for dear life to something and not moving forward because of my fear. Yet going through the fear is where *life* is.

A number of times in our conversations you asked me, "What is going on now?" In my responses, I returned to my head and just repeated some information. I sense that isn't what you were really asking. I think you were asking what I was feeling at that moment.

For example, a few hours after our last conversation, I had a heavy feeling that I sensed had to do with our conversation about the Eucharist. We laughed and joked about the Eucharist, but later I felt guilty about doing so in relation to a practice I once held as sacred. I think I was also feeling grief about leaving the Church, which was pivotal to my life for so many years. There was probably fear too.

Perhaps my real question is, can I really trust myself? Can I trust my intuitions and feelings? Can I trust the truth within myself? Yet I really believe I'm on the right path.

You keep reminding me that I'm God and that I don't need some other being or institution, even the Church, to tell me how to live. To regard myself as God is foreign to me. Yet in the core of my being I know it's true. I've been telling others we are one, and I believe the universe is one. I picture the universe as the murmuration of hundreds of flying birds that flow like waves but never run into each other.

The morning after this experience, I felt an opening within me, a lifting of a weight, a sense of freedom, and I had answers to my questions about the Eucharist.

So, I ask you, can you guide me in this?

Yeshua: You have said a great deal. I'd like to understand more about the shift that occurred the morning after our conversation. Did new understandings come through for you?

Tom: I guess the new understanding was that what you were saying is true. And my guilt was gone at that moment.

Yeshua: I'm happy for you. I am also pleased with the process you're describing. You opened to the feelings, or so it sounds to me. There were feelings of guilt, sadness, and fear, and you allowed them. It sounds like that process guided you, through your feelings, to a new place—a place of peace and resolution regarding your questions and an inner knowingness. Is that accurate?

Tom: Yes. Yes, it is.

Yeshua: That is a very good example of what it is to be your own authority, to follow your own guidance. It's often more about allowing than doing. You allowed the process, and it revealed itself.

Tom: Over the last few days I've had what I call a queasy feeling. I was dizzy and had brain fog. Finally, I sat down and asked myself, *Is there a word or picture or feeling that would describe all this?* Pretty soon a picture came, behind my eyelids, of the sun with flares or rays flowing outward. Then it turned into the night sky with violet energy lights around. I sat with that for a while. When I felt complete, I noticed the yucky feeling was gone.

Yeshua: Yes. So much of what humans do by tendency is to try to avoid, run away from, or change anything that feels unpleasant or uncomfortable. This can lead to many places, but it rarely leads to peace. To notice and be open to what you're experiencing is the Masculine process of being present.

The Feminine complement to this is to love. You could say that the Masculine, as presence, holds space. You might visualize this as a sacred circle that allows and is a container for Feminine love. This is part of the eternal dance between the Masculine and the Feminine, which you only discover when you stop running away.

Tom: I think I run away a lot.

Yeshua: [laughs] That's the third-dimensional MO, you could say. Running away can take endless forms, but the underlying fear that motivates the running is fundamentally the same. It's a fear of being devoured and obliterated by whatever is happening. Ultimately, it's fear of death. If you allow yourself to feel the fear, you'll notice it showing up moment to moment as long as you're in three-dimensional consciousness. This can be in the tiniest of ways, a simple worry or concern. There are endless forms, but it always comes down to survival.

Going Beyond the Third Dimension

Yeshua: My focus with humans at this time is to support a process that's often referred to as "ascension." This process is about going beyond the limits of the third dimension while harvesting the necessary soul gifts that beings come to the third dimension to receive. You might look at ascension as a kind of graduation. After completing the third dimension, you move on to the higher dimensions with the gifts you've received. With that will come many changes. A fundamental change is that you will no longer believe in dualistic reality, which seemed to be so real and true in the third dimension.

You will no longer believe in the dichotomy of life and death—thinking you have to run toward life and away from death. Instead, you will see the whole as something ongoing that simply changes form. That is a great shift. It's not simply an idea that can be believed and that will, therefore, transform you. It's a profound shift at the level of beingness that will be natural for you to make when you've completed your work in the third dimension.

Some who are following the spiritual path have tried to integrate this new perspective as a belief in the hope that belief would be enough. But it's not enough. Believing in oneness or unity can even be an obstacle to keep you from the real work you still have to do in the third dimension. Once you've completed that work, this new belief will be naturally supported. It will arise organically as a natural part of yourself, which is clear and obvious to you based on the growth you've undergone and who you are then.

So, it's not something you need to believe and try to conform your life to. Rather, it's something that may guide you, kind of like the north star. But in general, your focus needs to be on the next step that's right in front of you. For most people who are manifesting in the third dimension, their next step is still embedded in the third dimension. That's why you're here, to give you the opportunity to complete that work and have the growth your soul wants and needs, so you *can* move forward.

Tom: Yes, that's why I'm here. I think that's why I wanted to speak to you initially when I heard Mercedes channeling you and Mary Magdalene. Yet in the middle of it is fear. Sometimes I think, *If I really follow this path, am I going to have to let go of so many things? Will Ann disown me?* She's more evolved than I am, so I don't actually fear that because she's really supportive of me, but the fear remains.

Yeshua: Yes. This path is unknown, unfamiliar, so your fears are natural. They're also important and need to be addressed. What does the fear say you need? Do you need reassurance? Clarity about the process? Discernment about whether this is right for you or whether you're happy with what's occurring? These are just examples; it may be something else.

All fears are aspects of the fundamental fear of simply, fully, coming into this three-dimensional manifestation with the knowingness of the limits of the physical—that there can be suffering, pain, and death. To open to physical manifestation fully is a great part of what you and all beings came here to do. It's what you have not yet, for the most part, fully done.

Every moment of fear is an opportunity to open. As my beloved Mary Magdalene has described, not only do you have fear, you have a fear of fear. When you go beyond that secondary fear and open yourself to the fear, you will most likely be very surprised. It won't be what, at some level, you expect. On some level your being expects increased suffering or death.

Tom: We were taught that we *should be* suffering.

Yeshua: This is part of your religious training. This program was imposed on you to control you. But you did not come here to suffer

CAN I TRUST MYSELF? 105

because you have sinned. You came here to explore the Feminine, the great, amazing Feminine of God made manifest. When I say you are God, I absolutely see you as God, but so is everything else. All of manifestation is God, including all physical forms. What a wonder! What a miracle!

Humans came here to explore their godly capacity for free will and creation and to learn the lessons of that. You're learning how to use free will, how to relate to free will in others, and how to create on the basis of free will in ways that are fulfilling for you and for others. This is God-training.

How God Views Killing

Tom: Regarding free will, what puzzles me is shootings. How does God view killing someone?

Yeshua: Since you are God, how do you view killing?

Tom: To me it shouldn't happen.

Yeshua: But why?

Tom: It's taking someone else's life. At the same time, I think, *Maybe both of those people chose that.*

Yeshua: They did indeed choose it. But that doesn't negate your feelings, thoughts, or conclusions about it. They're not exclusive of each other.

Tom: My wife and I spent three years in the Holy Land in Jerusalem. While there, we heard about the Holocaust—how terrible things were and the destruction of so many lives. I'm puzzled by what happened and who was really behind it. Was the Church part of it?

Yeshua: You were behind it all.

Tom: I was behind it all?

Yeshua: Yes.

Tom: I guess, since it's part of my story, I must have chosen that.

Yeshua: Yes. This is part of what humans came here to explore: giving life and taking life in many forms. And to learn and grow from that.

On some level you like the idea of being one with everyone, but do you like the idea of being one with Hitler?

Tom: No.

Yeshua: Do you like the idea of being one with the Nazis?

Tom: No.

Yeshua: So, are you only one with the people you like?

Tom: I guess I am, even though I say I am one with the universe.

Yeshua: I disagree. I would say you are one with all of it. This is why when you ask "Who is behind it?" I say, "You." You will grow enormously if you let that in.

It's also true that you are only manifesting as you. As a distinct and unique individual, you have free will, as does everyone else.

Thus, it's also true that you have chosen *not* to act like Hitler and the Nazis. These things are simultaneously true. You are an individuated, unique manifestation, and you are non-separate from all. *And both are God.*

When you move into the fourth dimension, you will see that you have the power to create your reality. You will see that you've always had this power. You have created your reality all along. At a certain point, this understanding will lead you to take responsibility for all the reality you've created. But this is most likely not your concern right now because this is not what is real for you. What I hear is real for you is that you are disturbed because you see life as sacred, and you want it protected and valued rather than destroyed and damaged. Is this accurate?

Tom: Yes. As you speak, I realize that I'm judgmental about a lot of things.

Yeshua: Yes, yes.

Tom: I'm judgmental because of my experience in the Holy Land. The Palestinians are being pushed down. I guess I'm on both sides there too. I want to blame Netanyahu for what he's doing, but I have to be careful because I'm part of that too.

Yeshua: Rather than going into blame, go into pain. Blame is still the third-dimensional program, which revolves around who's right and who's wrong. Pain is your truth, your reality, and your compass. You can say, "I'm in pain when I hear about the suffering and pain both sides are experiencing." Then you don't need to blame. This will lead you to what you really want: support for life, cooperation, harmony, and much more, I imagine.

Tom: Yes, yes.

Yeshua: Doing that will empower you to create a different reality on many levels. The most powerful level is consciousness.

Tom: When I said I have to change how I see the Jews as the chosen people, you said, "You can do that if you want, but it won't necessarily liberate you. It will just replace one belief with another set of beliefs based on the exact same consciousness."

Yeshua: Yes. Your motivation to change was coming from the underlying belief that it would be wrong to see the Jews as the chosen people and that you needed to change that belief to one that's right. But you were still coming from a paradigm of right and wrong.

Tom: That's right [laughs]. One of these days I'll get it.

Yeshua: What was your deeper motivation beneath the idea that you need to change your belief that the Jews are the chosen people? What was really motivating you to say that?

Tom: I believe God would not choose one being or group over others. We're all important to God. We're all one with God. We're all equal in God.

Yeshua: Yes. It sounds like when you hear the belief that the Jews are the chosen people, you feel doubt. That doubt is pointing you to a greater reality—you could say a greater understanding or perspective—that all people are equally valuable, and the God *you* know would not choose some over others. There's no need, and it isn't of value to do that.

Rather than replacing one belief with another, you move to a higher level, a higher reality, a higher consciousness. This is similar to the quote from Einstein that a problem can never be solved at the same level it was created. At that higher level, there is the knowingness of valuing all equally. This isn't a rule of how people should be related to. It's simply an inherent understanding. You might look at it as something like valuing a lion and a lamb equally. They're not equal in the sense of sameness—they're very different—but their value is inherently equal.

Tom: That's how God sees it, and that's how I want to see it.

Yeshua: Yes. Out of that comes compassion. From that higher perspective, when you hear the idea that the Jews are the chosen people, you respond with compassion rather than argument or conflict, such as, *No, they're not the chosen people! That's wrong!* That kind of negation points to the consciousness that's still residing at the same level. When you move to the higher level, it shifts your whole relationship to the original idea. Can you feel that?

Tom: Yes.

Yeshua: Yes.

The Feminine Guidance System

Tom: If doubts arise, that's what I have to stay with.

Yeshua: I would recommend it.

Tom: When I was part of the Church, I had a lot of doubts, but I didn't trust them.

Yeshua: You were taught not to trust them. This is part of the authoritarian model. You are slowly reclaiming yourself and your wholeness, your guidance system, your connection to your higher self. One of the greatest tools and supports for doing that is your feelings. Doubt is a feeling. You can feel it in your body when you doubt something, right?

Tom: Yes.

Yeshua: Yes. It's an actual feeling. It's valuable. It's information. It's a support for you to listen to and receive that guidance.

Tom: That's what you described as following the Feminine.

Yeshua: Yes because feelings are part of the Feminine.

Tom: What does it really mean to follow the Feminine?

Yeshua: It means to follow your body, your feelings, and your energy. It includes your sexuality. All of that is following the Feminine, which ultimately leads to following the heart. The heart is the seat of the Divine Feminine within all beings, just as the mind is the seat of the Masculine.

Most of you have learned to live from your mind and to run from the Feminine. A tiny bit of the Feminine may squeak through on rare occasions because perhaps you haven't been successful in obliterating all of it [laughs]. Let us hope.

Tom: Sexuality especially has had such a bad rap over the years.

Yeshua: Of course, because it's part of the Feminine. It was an easy target, which has had devastating consequences.

Tom: There's a lot of fear about it.

Yeshua: Absolutely. And estrangement from your body, your feelings, and ultimately yourself. You were indoctrinated into the authoritarian beliefs that sexuality was sinful and evil. I would say those beliefs and that system are much more sinful and evil than sexuality ever was because they separated you from yourself, from God, from your world, from each other. What could be more sinful than that?

Tom: And that's what we came here to learn.

Yeshua: Yes. The path was not preordained. It's been a creative process as to how it has unfolded, and it continues to be.

Tom: That's why Ann and I want to learn Mary Magdalene's Heart Path.[22]

Yeshua: This is why my beloved Mary was so passionate and moved to bring this to people—to help you rectify this great imbalance that has been created in yourselves and in your world. Most of you are so estranged from the Feminine and so locked into the Masculine. She brought this through because she desires so much to help. She wants you to have all your gifts, talents, blessings, and faculties, which has everything to do with re-embracing, getting to know, and becoming mature and strong in the Feminine.

This is not to negate the Masculine. It's to come into *balance* with the Masculine. Doing so will change a great deal for all of you and your world.

Many people in the spiritual world have the desire to ascend. What they're generally envisioning is a move to other places, other dimensions, other realities. People talk about the fourth dimension, the fifth dimension, the sixth dimension, and even higher. Yes, these are wonderful places, but that is not why you came here. Everyone incarnate here came here to receive the lessons, blessings, and gifts of the third dimension.

Most individuals would support the process of ascension much more by opening themselves to this pathway of learning what the Feminine is. Learn what it is to open to, embrace, include, and cherish the Feminine rather than escaping to higher dimensions. The escape is like watching TV or having a drink. It lasts for a while, and then you come back until you've completed the work here [laughs]. When you've completed your work, you organically graduate and move to the next level.

Pleasure as Celebration of God

Tom: You mentioned watching TV. Ann and I seldom watch TV, especially the news, which is often more about violence than anything else.

Yeshua: Why do you think that is?

Tom: They want to put fear into people.

Yeshua: I don't think they need to *put* fear into people. They want to reinforce fear in people [laughs].

Tom: Recently, while watching a hockey game, I felt guilty. *I should be reading our conversations rather than watching the game,* I thought. Then I countered with, *I can watch the hockey game. It's not that I'm excluding our work.* Every once in a while though I have those pangs of guilt.

Yeshua: If you're a sinner who has been suffering from original sin even before you incarnated, you can't afford a moment of pleasure, can you? Especially knowing that pleasure is based in the Feminine [laughs].

Look at it from another perspective. As you watch the hockey game, you're experiencing the joy and excitement of what human beings are capable of: skill, mastery, beauty, cooperation. So many parts to watching a game can give you tremendous pleasure.

You can relate to all of life with pleasure—that is, if you're not busy atoning for some sin that someone said you have to spend your life fixing [laughs]. You're really celebrating God in that particular form: through the mastery of those players, their skill, their interaction with the elements in all its beauty—the ice, the skates, the human body—all of that. So much to celebrate.

Tom: Unfortunately, there's a lot of fighting too.

Yeshua: Yes, and that part may be less enjoyable. At some point the fighting may be a reason why you choose not to watch hockey. But there will be other ways of enjoying the pleasurable qualities of the sport that do not include fighting.

Tom: Yes, that's right.

I have another question about Scripture. Based on what's recorded in the Bible, we really don't know much about you. Are there other books or gospels that tell more of who you really were?

Yeshua: What do you need to know about me?

Tom: There's a period of about eighteen years during which we don't know where you were. What kinds of studies did you go through? Mary Magdalene talks about being in Egypt in the mystery schools. Did you go there?

Yeshua: Of course I did [laughs]. Why would I not have?

Tom: Those are long distances. You traveled a long way.

Yeshua: I had help. I was helped, trained, and supported by masters of the time. There were many in many places. The period of time you're talking about was my natural time of growth and learning. My training and travels were also to bless and exchange my gifts with others. But that span of time was primarily to prepare me for the work I came to do.

I traveled in Egypt, India, and in what was called Persia. I also traveled to parts of Europe. I had contact with those beyond India in Tibet and Nepal. The Church was very selective about what they did or didn't include in the Bible, based on what they thought would most support their agenda. From their point of view, my travels during that part of my life did not support their intentions and motivations, so they weren't included, though they were never secret.

Tom: Yet when you came back from the various countries and cultures, the Bible says you were faced with great opposition. People didn't accept what you were teaching.

Yeshua: The opposition wasn't because I had spent time in other places. It was simply because I was challenging the status quo and what people believed. People were very attached to those beliefs and fearful of giving them up. I was also challenging the power structure. Those who were benefiting from the power structure were averse to changing that structure and giving up their power. All that was part of a great play of learning in the third dimension for everyone involved.

Tom: I'm sorry you had to go through that.

Yeshua: It was not the most fun journey I've ever been on. [Yeshua and Tom chuckle.] Nor the easiest.

Tom: I'm sure.

Yeshua: Yet there was much that was beautiful, much that was undeniably infused with God—and part of *my* soul path as well.

Tom: Did you know before you came that you would be experiencing all this?

Yeshua: I knew to the degree I could know. Actually experiencing it was a different thing.

Tom: Your mother, Mary, and Mary Magdalene went through a great deal too. They must have experienced great pain.

Yeshua: Absolutely, and many others as well. The third dimension is a painful place, paired with incredible ecstasy and joy. The whole spectrum is included here. It's all a possibility and a reality at various times in everyone's life.

Tom: Thank you for being who you are and for what you did. I hope I can be of some help in what you came to do.

Yeshua: The help you can offer is to become what I modeled—and more. This is the greatest contribution anyone can make. From that place it's natural to hear your guidance as to what your particular contribution is, which may look nothing like mine, but that is of little consequence. In many ways the process is the same for all, just as there are similarities for every human being in the process of being born and going through the stages of childhood, adulthood, old age, and death.

There are many universals, both in the human life cycle and in the process of spiritual growth and development. Yet each individual form is incredibly unique. I modeled something as someone further along the path, but it's the same path for all and the same essential process that everyone will go through. You will have your individual way of going through it, and it will lead you to your individual gifts as well as the contribution that is uniquely yours.

Tom: And a big help is to follow our emotions.

Yeshua: Yes. A big help is to include the Feminine [laughs]. Emotions are a big part of that. Your world is awakening to this.

Tom: Yes.

Yeshua: Recently in your world, women have been coming forth and expressing publicly the ways they've been hurt by the Masculine.[23] Men are going through a process too, struggling to hear and receive their words and their hurt. This is an indication of the great awakening that your world is on the precipice of. You're starting to understand that the Feminine is different from the Masculine. You're starting to discover what that difference is and how to relate to the Feminine differently from what has been done in the past, which has hurt men and women.

Tom: I believe you said that to cut the Feminine out is to cut out part of ourselves.

Yeshua: [chuckles] A huge part. It's cutting out manifestation. It's cutting out life. Really, it's cutting out birth, life, and death.

Tom: Thank you so much, Yeshua, for hanging in there with me.

Yeshua: Thank you for hanging in there with me.

The Inner Judge

Yeshua: Are there more questions? Are there more unresolved feelings, thoughts? I would love to hear them.

Tom: Can I trust my intuition?

Yeshua: You've probably been trained not to trust it. The first step to changing that is to become aware of your training regarding intuition. Notice whether that training is supporting you or not and whether you want to continue to hold on to that training.

The primary way to find out whether you can trust your intuition is experience. When you have an intuition, and you follow it, what's your experience? When you don't follow your intuition, what's your experience? Observing your experience in these ways is how you'll find out whether you can trust your intuition. Have you already noticed what happens when you follow your intuition?

Tom: I have.

Yeshua: What has been the result?

Tom: It's been OK.

Yeshua: [laughs] And yet there's still a question of whether or not it's OK.

Tom: Yes. As I've said, it was a major step for me to leave the priesthood. I haven't been shot down or anything.

Yeshua: But that programming was internalized as part of your internal judge or inner authority, which says, *Maybe it hasn't happened yet, but you're still in danger. You're still doing the wrong thing.* This program is insidious. Become aware of when the program is popping up, and start to practice discernment. *Oh, that's the program. Do I still want to hold on to that program? Is it serving me or not?* Then you can exercise choice.

Tom: You recommended I ask "Does it lead me to love myself more?" when I asked about being a vegetarian. I could ask that question here too.

Yeshua: Yes, yes. A litmus test is to ask, "Is this increasing love and light in my life?" If it is, I would say it is supportive. If it's not, I would say it's not supportive.

Tom: Yes. And you said if I'm judging someone or some situation, I can't send love and light. I can only send the energy of my contracted self, which is fear.

Yeshua: [chuckles] Yes, and your mind-generated ideas of rightness and wrongness, which is what people tend to use as artillery against each other.

Tom: Even though I wasn't happy when I left the priesthood, I can't be hard on the Church.

Yeshua: Oh, you can be if you want [laughs]. But I doubt that is going to increase love and light in your life [more laughter].

Tom: When I heard that Jesus is not in the Eucharist, my first reaction was to say, "So, forget it then." But I guess I can't do that.

Yeshua: God is in everything.

What is more to the point is that your involvement in the Church—doing certain practices and holding on to certain beliefs—wasn't supporting you in your realization of God. Rather than third-dimensional, dualistic thinking—this is true or not true. Jesus is here, or Jesus is not here—go to the higher level: is this supporting me in the path of uniting with God? The beliefs and practice you held earlier in your life probably were supporting you at that time. I hope they did, at least to some extent. I'm imagining you reached a place where the answer to that question—of whether those beliefs and practices were supporting you—had become, *No, not enough. Not as much as I want.*

Tom: That's right.

Yeshua: There still might have been aspects of your life as a priest that were supporting your higher being: the people you connected with from the heart, perhaps the ceremony (which many people love about the Catholic Church), the community, the stability, structure, form, and even the security. Those things may have been wonderful, or at least parts of them. But being supported in some ways doesn't mean the whole package was ultimately supporting you.

Tom: That's right. I'm thinking I can ask this question with many things: is it leading me to love or not to love?

Yeshua: Yes. For those who are still in the Church, their involvement is probably supporting their soul path and soul choices—until it's not. Being involved in the Church doesn't make someone lower, lesser, or behind anyone else. Everyone's soul path is different. Respect that soul path.

Tom: We all have our own path to follow.

Yeshua: Indeed. You can still have feelings and thoughts about what others are doing, which you may or may not choose to express. Your feelings and thoughts might include that you don't like something, that it's painful for you, or that you question it. That's not the same as saying, "This is wrong. This is bad. This is not the truth."

Tom: I think this might be a place to stop for today.

Yeshua: Exactly what I was thinking [laughs].

Tom: Thank you so much for this, Yeshua.

Yeshua: You are welcome. I wish to offer you a blessing if that is something you would like.

Tom: Yes, very much so. Thank you.

Yeshua: Then let us end with this blessing. [A period of silence follows as Yeshua offers his blessing.]

In God's light and love, I thank you and embrace you. Blessings, beloved brother.

Tom: Thank you. Blessings to you.

SEVEN

Sexuality and Brainwashing

Yeshua: Hello, beloved. It is I, Yeshua, once again. I'm happy to return and be with you. Please share with me what is in your heart and mind today that I may help with.

Tom: Thank you, Yeshua. Thanks for coming back.

Yeshua: You're welcome.

Tom: I appreciate our last conversation, particularly your remarks about doubt, which I experience so often. You said doubt is part of my guidance system and that it would benefit me to listen and receive that guidance. So often it seemed that others were smarter than me and that they had the truth. Thank you for teaching me how to follow my doubts to lead me to my own authority and truth.

Today, I have a question about sexuality. For me, sexuality conjures up a lot of feelings. Over the years I've carried a lot of beliefs and baggage about sexuality. Particularly in the Church, sexuality has had a bad rap.

I'd like to go back to our conversation about the Eucharist. I mentioned how we'd been instructed to masticate the bread, and you responded, "Maybe they meant masturbate." I immediately had a strong feeling of wrongness. I was shocked and disturbed that you used that word and keep asking myself, *Why did you?*

Yeshua: Would you like me to respond to that?

Tom: Yes. I might not get to my real question, but OK.

Yeshua: Is this not a real question?

Tom: It is a real question. [Yeshua and Tom laugh.] But I keep trying to get to my agenda.

Yeshua: Well, should we go with your agenda, or should we go with your heart?

Tom: Let's go with my heart.

Yeshua: [laughs] I support that choice. I have been waiting for you to ask about this.

Tom: [laughs] I wanted to, but I was hesitant.

Yeshua: Yes. I said that intentionally, for many reasons. We were addressing your feelings about the Eucharist, and you were lightening up to the point that we were enjoying ourselves and laughing as we shared about that.

Tom: Yes, yes.

Yeshua: To me that was a sign that your heart was opening. I was glad about that. You see, the Eucharist is an example of so much that the Church has done. They've taken my words and actions out of context and put a whole different spin on them. I never intended that there should be this kind of ritual, which is looked at as some kind of magical ceremony and presented as unquestionable. It's like a magic totem that you can't be light about; you have to be heavy and serious. And it's given its own authority over you. Do you understand what I'm saying?

Tom: Yes, yes.

Yeshua: This heavy, ritualistic orientation to the Eucharist was all created by the Church. I never turned the Eucharist into some kind of holy ceremony where you're going to go to hell if you make a joke about it. [Yeshua and Tom laugh.] I never even talked about hell! [Yeshua laughs.] Another creation by the Church. There are so many.

What I was so pleased about was your joy, lightness, and humor as we were engaging. To me these were signs you were shaking off the tyranny of the fear-based indoctrination that you had received. Do you see? You were made to believe that you should stand in fear of the holy Eucharist, and if you don't, you'll be damned. Am I correct?

Tom: Yes. To kneel down too.

Yeshua: Yes. What has that got to do with me? With God? With anything? I never taught that the practice was to be in fear. I never talked about punishment. That was not my teaching. My teaching was about love. Love of God; love of one another.

Stating that my body is the bread was saying that I am in *all* life, not that I'm going to be reduced to some wafer that can only be distributed by the high muckety-muck and with a certain kind of dance that you have to do. And if you do it wrong, too bad. You're damned [laughs.] That's the *opposite* of what I intended.

What I was saying was no different from what other traditions have said, certainly the Goddess tradition of that time. The celebration of bread and wine is a symbol or representation of life. I was teaching to see me in *all* of life and to relate to *all* of life as me. The beliefs associated with the Eucharist have misrepresented this understanding, limiting me to this little wafer and this sip of something or other. And you'd better get it right because everything else is hell and damnation! [laughs]

I laugh because it's my nature to laugh. But I am sad for you and for so many who have believed such things. From my point of view, this teaching about the Eucharist is a great detour from the path I want to support.

This is similar to what you learned about sexuality. You learned that sexuality was evil and sinful. When did I ever say that? When did that ever have anything to do with what I taught? Yet it's considered one of the foundations of Roman Catholicism, if not all of Christianity—in my name. But that was not my relationship to sexuality or to so many things.

I have no sense that sexuality is evil, wrong, or sinful. That was not my teaching. These negative judgments were added for very different reasons that have to do with power and control. To be blunt about it, I would say the Church's teaching about sexuality was used to brainwash people with fear. And that brainwashing has been very effective. Yet you, Tom, have managed to break away from the brainwashing. Your own feelings and thoughts were slipping through the cracks, just enough for you to be able to access and make use of those capacities. You could no longer accept the overlay that had covered so much.

You could say that you've come out of the brainwashing. Yet it's like you have flashbacks. There are times when the old programming wells up: *Oh, no, no, no! That's wrong. You can't make a joke about masturbation when we're talking about the holy Eucharist* [laughs].

Tom: Yes. Can you speak about masturbation and how you see it?

Yeshua: To me it's a simple thing. It's a celebration of life. It's a celebration of the body, which is divine, and of your sexuality, which is divine. It's certainly not a sin or something that's going to send you to hell, if there were such a place [laughs]. You've been sold a pack of lies. What could be so evil about masturbation? Please explain to me how you see masturbation [laughs.]

Tom: The training I received was that anything to do with sexuality had to be for procreation only. Don't look, don't touch. In fact, the Church took on God's authority, your authority, and they had control over every aspect of sexuality: marriage, celibacy, relationships, contraception, sexual orientation, separation, and divorce.

Yeshua: I understand this. My question is, why? What does that serve? What truth is in that?

Tom: It serves authority.

Yeshua: Yes, and in particular, the Masculine authority [laughs]. This is not exclusive to men but to the Masculine that wants to eradicate the Feminine. What's so bad about sexuality? If you strip away what you were taught, what do you see?

Tom: Pleasure, beauty.

Yeshua: And what's so bad about that?

Tom: There's nothing wrong with pleasure. It's good, as a matter of fact. [Tom and Yeshua laugh.]

Yeshua: Absolutely. It's part of this world and part of the Feminine in particular. The Church's position toward sexuality has been all about power and control—a brilliant strategy to take away your humanity and your divinity and most certainly to take away the power of the Feminine. Then you become easy to control.

Sexuality Is Sacred

Tom: If sexuality is part of the Feminine, are we supposed to follow our sexuality? What does that mean? Is it like following emotions? Do they all lead to God?

Yeshua: You should have been taught skills, techniques, and wisdom regarding these things instead of the ridiculousness you were taught. In its simplest form, following means neither suppressing nor denying.

But there is much beyond that. When sexuality is seen as more than a physical or biological act, you start to see it as a sacred and spiritual act. That's a great blessing, a great gift. There are skills to be learned as to how to relate to sexuality in a sacred way. Very few in your world know about sacred sexuality, so you must seek it out. Some people understand and share this with others, but most people are oblivious to this possibility.

That is unfortunate. It would be so much better for all if the understanding and skills of sacred sexuality were understood by everyone. It would be better if children learned sacred sexuality from their parents—and I don't mean any kind of invasion of the child's sexuality. I simply mean the way parents educate children for what they need to learn as they grow into adulthood.

At a deeper level, opening to sacred sexuality requires you to understand and release your fear of the Feminine. In practicing sacred sexuality, you realize that your growth, evolution, and spiritual development depend on opening to the Feminine and receiving the gifts of the Feminine.

This kind of valuing has been realized to a huge extent with regard to the Masculine in the arenas of mind, willpower, achievement, goal setting, and goal accomplishment. There is just as much for you to learn and receive that is absolutely essential in the Feminine arena. The ignoring of the Feminine must change.

To follow the Feminine is to allow the Feminine to lead, to teach you, and to start to make you whole. Then the Feminine can join in combination with the Masculine. This is the way for individuals as well as for your world altogether. Your world is suffering tremendously through being locked into the Masculine in separation from the Feminine. Certainly, the Church is a strong bastion of that separation.

Tom: Hmm . . .

Yeshua: Does that answer your question?

Tom: Yes, it does.

Yeshua: So, let's go back to masturbation. I'm not saying everyone should masturbate multiple times a day, randomly, whenever they want, wherever they want. I'm saying that masturbation isn't a sin; it's part of your beautiful humanity. And there is skill that goes with it.

Ultimately, masturbation is a sacred sexual practice when engaged appropriately and with the right understanding and skill. Then it isn't called masturbation. It's often called *solo practice*. This term points to a different understanding than what most people think of when they hear the word "masturbation." For most people, masturbation is associated with stimulating yourself to the point of orgasm and release. It's what beings do when they're limited to their biology and instinctual drives. But there is so much more to be received and given through sexuality. This requires education, practice, and the development of higher skills and pathways. This I wish for all of you.

Tom: Yes, I wish for that too. Thank you for talking about this with me. It wasn't easy to ask the question.

Yeshua: Yes. That's an example and indication of that old programming still running. *You can't talk about that! That's wrong. And if you do, you should experience guilt for having done it, maybe even shame for having done it.* All of that old programming has yet to be completely purified.

Tom: Thank you.

Opening to Pleasure

Tom: I want to talk more about pleasure and sexuality. I spoke before about feeling guilty about watching a hockey game, like it was a waste of time. Part of me was thinking I should be doing something more in line with promoting ascension or raising my vibration, as though there's an agenda to fulfill, and I'm not doing my job. In response, you spoke of joy and pleasure at seeing the movement, the skating, the body, the intricacy, and the cooperation. I think I have issues with pleasure, just enjoying and simply drinking in the moment. It's as if I shouldn't be feeling it; I should be doing something else or be somewhere else.

Yeshua: I'm guessing that you were taught from an early age that pleasure was evil, sinful, and something to feel guilty about. Is this accurate?

Tom: I'm not sure that's totally accurate. I don't remember being deliberately told that pleasure was sinful or awful. Somewhere along the line though I must've picked up that there are things that need to be done, and I should be doing them. If I'm not, if I'm enjoying myself, I'm not doing what I should.

Yeshua: Where do you think you picked this up?

Tom: From Church maybe or from family. One thing I think about is that my father never played games with us as a child.

Yeshua: Mm-hmm. So, somehow, you got the idea that there were certain things that were valuable to spend your time doing.

Tom: Yes.

Yeshua: And certain things that were a waste of time.

Tom: Yeah.

Yeshua: That was indoctrinated into you, either overtly or covertly. You can receive indoctrination from observing and learning what everyone else is doing.

Tom: Mm-hmm.

Yeshua: I assume that working in some fashion or other was considered valuable, and experiencing pleasure was considered a waste of time?

Tom: Yes.

Yeshua: So you're still carrying out that program. Do you see that working to achieve goals is the Masculine and pleasure is the Feminine? That training says that the Masculine is valuable and worthy of your time and energy and that the Feminine is not valuable and a waste of your time and energy.

Tom: That's right.

Yeshua: What do you experience when you devote yourself solely to accomplishing goals and do not allow yourself pleasure?

Tom: I guess I experience some sadness.

Yeshua: What are you sad about?

Tom: I want to feel joy. To feel happy. To experience laughter.

Yeshua: Yes. Those feed you and help keep you balanced and whole.
This is part of the indoctrination that creates a worker-bee mentality for most of humanity: *Your life should be about work, work, work; accomplish, accomplish, accomplish.* This is a program that someone or some group is running on you—those who are

benefiting from all your labor and your lack of wholeness. They benefit from your labor in obvious ways. They benefit from your lack of wholeness in that you're inherently depriving yourself of your own strength and power, so it's easy for them to dominate you and continue to milk you for all you're worth. Does that make sense to you?

Tom: Yes. I think that was more so in the past than in the present.

Yeshua: Good [laughs]. Congratulations!

Tom: Can I tell you a bit about my sabbatical?

Yeshua: If that is what's coming up for you, and you have questions about it, most certainly.

Tom: I was in the Holy Land with twenty-one people visiting sites where supposedly you had been. What was most impactful for me was our group decision making about how we would celebrate the Eucharist, given the interdenominational nature of our group.

One day a non-Catholic priest led the Eucharist, and I had a real dilemma. As everyone else went to receive communion, I felt somehow that I, as a Catholic priest, couldn't go. I was representing the Church, and Catholics are not allowed to receive communion at a non-Catholic celebration. I felt really bad about that. All the other Catholic members of our group participated, but I didn't. I spent the rest of the day by myself, asking, *What am I trying to preserve? What is going on here?* I nearly became ill over the whole thing.

At the end of our trip, those in charge of the liturgy said, "Tom, we know where you've stood, but we would like you and the Episcopalian bishop to co-celebrate a Eucharist." Now, in my tradition, that was a no-no. But as I thought about it, what came to me was, *We're walking in the footsteps of Jesus. He would want us to celebrate this together.* So, I said, "Yes, I will." And I did. I felt really good that we could celebrate the Eucharist together. That was the beginning of my breaking from the Church.

Afterward I toured Europe. I went to many holy places where people have had wonderful experiences, but I didn't feel happy or joyful at those places, and I wondered why.

Yeshua: It's not just that you *weren't* having happy experiences. You were having *another* experience, and you weren't connected to your real experience. In a global kind of way, you might say you were having unhappy feelings. Or maybe you were having neutral feelings. It's not clear. When you say what you're *not* experiencing, no one knows what you *are* experiencing. Perhaps you didn't know what you were experiencing.

What was important was what you *were* experiencing, not what you weren't experiencing [laughs]. You're always having feelings, and you're always having an experience. What you *were* experiencing was your actual gift. But you were thinking you should've had a different gift.

Tom: Yes.

Yeshua: So you missed your gift—that's the real tragedy. The feelings you were having were perfect for you.

I would certainly say you were divorced from your feelings when you initially chose not to participate in the Eucharist with the other participants in your program. Your response was overwritten by your beliefs and indoctrination, so what you did was not in line with your feelings.

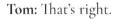

Tom: That's right.

Yeshua: You wanted to join them in celebrating their expression and love of God and to share your expression and love of God.

Tom: Yes.

Yeshua: And I would say you *were* connected to your feelings when you accepted the invitation at the end of the program and said, "Yes, I will do this." It sounds like you were glad you made that choice. Doing so allowed you to participate, and you were happy with the event that took place. But even more so, you were happy about your own growth and liberation, in being connected to yourself and having the courage to follow your truth versus your indoctrination.

Tom: I was told later that I could have been excommunicated [laughs]. That might've been easier for me [more laughter].

Yeshua: That might have been a gift too.

Tom: Yes.

Yeshua: Might have at least sped up your process of leaving the Church.

Tom: That's right.

After that I went to California for the rest of my sabbatical. I participated in several Church-oriented courses. I also took a dream workshop, which really helped me in my decision making. It was then that I chose to leave the priesthood.

The icing on the cake was reconnecting with Ann in California. Since I married Ann, I've been more in touch with my experiences in relationships and nature. She's someone who goes into ecstasy over a child, a flower, a sunset, a moon, or an oak tree. She sees beauty everywhere, and I marvel at her. We'll be eating a meal, and she'll say, "Look, look! Look at the bird." Or we'll be driving along, and she'll say, "Look at that!" The joy within her has taught me about joy and happiness. I'm really gifted to have her in my life.

Yeshua: So, what is your question?

Tom: Sometimes I still go back to the program that tells me I should be doing something other than just enjoying the moment.

Yeshua: How can I help you?

Tom: You have helped me through speaking about the Feminine and going into the Feminine. I'm learning to experience the joy and the gifts of the Feminine.

Yeshua: This is what you came here to learn.

Tom: Yes, yes. So, I have to enjoy that. No, I choose to enjoy that [laughs].

Yeshua: I suggest that you open yourself to whatever your experience is. If you long for joy, open yourself to that. If you long to be productive and to accomplish something, open yourself to that.

You have a deep distrust of yourself. As part of your indoctrination, you can't trust yourself. So, you need authorities to tell you what to do. Once you're sufficiently indoctrinated, their system lives within your brain, and you're constantly carrying out the dictates of your indoctrination. Part of that system was not to trust yourself and instead trust the program. Yes?

Tom: Yes, yes.

Yeshua: You have done tremendous work with this. The fact that you chose to leave the priesthood and get married is *huge* evidence that you are trusting yourself more strongly than you do the programs that were fed to you. I congratulate you on that.

Tom: Thank you. And with your support and assistance, I'll continue. You've been so supportive of me.

Yeshua: I love you.

Tom: Thank you.

Yeshua: You are my brother. You are my friend. You are my soul companion.

Tom: It touches my heart when you say that.

Yeshua: Good. And we are all the family of God. How are you in this moment?

Tom: I have peace inside.

Yeshua: Wonderful.

Tom: Part of me is asking, *Should I continue with my agenda?* But I don't want to do that. I want to stay with the peace [laughs].

Yeshua: Yes, yes.

Finding Your Soul Path

Yeshua: So, within this peace, are there any questions that remain for today?

Tom: In our last conversation, you told me, "The help you can offer is to become what I modeled, and more." How did you do your modeling when you were incarnated?

Yeshua: It's not so much that I was doing modeling. It's that I was doing my work, and that is a model for all of you.

Tom: Mm-hmm.

Yeshua: Ultimately, it's as simple as being in communion with God, both the Feminine and the Masculine side, Mother God and Father God. Out of that fullness of communion, your task is to discover what your path is, your contribution, which all people have. That path supports your communion with God and helps to grow it. This is your soul path.

Tom: Hmm . . .

Yeshua: Within that there is also the element of contribution. That means to discover and engage your contribution. That's a description of what I modeled. The path is the same in a broad way—painted with broad strokes—for everyone. Is that helpful?

Tom: It is. If I'm going to follow your modeling, I need to be in communion with God, both the Masculine and the Feminine, and then use my gifts.

Yeshua: And it's up to you to find *your* way of being in communion with God, which supports you the most, and which may not look at all like my way. And that is of little consequence.

Tom: Hmm . . .

Yeshua: The communion with God is what's important.

Tom: Mm-hmm. I guess part of me wants to hear what you did. As you were growing up, did you have fun? Did you play soccer? [laughs]

Yeshua: [laughs] I had great fun, great joy, and great delight. This is part of why I enjoy children so much. I can relate to them directly in terms of joy and happiness. It's a very direct heart connection.

Tom: It moves my heart to witness families enjoying each other, with children playing.

Yeshua: Yes.

Tom: Occasionally, when I experience families not getting along, maybe arguing, it really bothers me. But I guess that's their path.

Yeshua: It may or it may not be. It is to some extent because it's manifesting. Whether they're responding in the most productive way is not clear.

Tom: Yes. There's joy in seeing children being free to play and have fun.

Yeshua: Yes. It's a sign of their communion in the moment, which you feel directly.

Tom: Yes. In our conversations you have laughed a lot, but I've always pictured you as more serious.

Yeshua: That's how the Church has portrayed me.

Tom: Although in the Bible you went to a lot of meals. You ate a lot, with a lot of people. [Yeshua laughs heartily.] That's all Jesus ever did was to sit and eat. [Tom laughs.]

Yeshua: [laughs] But probably with no pleasure. [Tom laughs.]

Championing the Feminine

Tom: When they speak of the wedding at Cana, was that your wedding?

Yeshua: Absolutely.

Tom: It was?

Yeshua: Of course. Why should I not be married?

Tom: I'm glad you were married.

Yeshua: [laughs] Yes, you have discovered the joys and benefits— the great benefit.

Tom: That's right. Thank you for telling me that.

Yeshua: I imagine that brings relief for you.

Tom: Yes.

Yeshua: Reassurance of the choices you have made.

Tom: Yes. I heard you had children; is that correct?

Yeshua: Of course I had children. Why would I not have children? And why wouldn't I want children?

Tom: Hmm . . .

Yeshua: *All* of that is God. All of that is the path of communion with God, despite the stories and beliefs that others have put forth. This is what I came to model.

Tom: Hmm . . . And, Mary Magdalene worked along with you?

Yeshua: Of course [laughs]. She's a greatly advanced soul and my beloved helpmate. Why would she not?

Tom: Yes.

Yeshua: The truth is, the world needed her teaching more than mine. But it wasn't ready.

Tom: Hmm . . .

Yeshua: So, my work, which is part of the great work of the Masculine, is to protect her and to help the world see her gifts. To see her beauty, her divinity. Because I see that as her lover.

Tom: Hmm . . .

Yeshua: My job is to create the circumstances and the space for her to shine, for her to be seen as the beautiful God-being, the miraculous, wondrous, Divine Feminine that she is. Then she can simply be that, from which we all benefit. Do you understand?

Tom: Yes. It sounds so good.

Yeshua: It is so good [laughs]. Take my word for it [more laughter.] Sadly, so few in your world realize it. But it is coming. It is time. The platform is laid. The Masculine is beginning to understand its role relative to the Feminine and the amazing, tremendous benefit of doing that.

Tom: To open to the Feminine.

Yeshua: To *champion* the Feminine. To *adore* the Feminine. And to be the protector and promoter of the Feminine. Opening to the Feminine is the internal work of the Masculine. That's the preparatory work. But the fullness is to champion the Feminine.

Tom: Thank you.

Yeshua: You are welcome.

One of my greatest celebrations of my lifetime on Earth is that I united with my beloved Mary Magdalene in human form. To the extent that I was able, I was her beloved Masculine—supporting her, championing her, receiving her gifts, and, of course, helping her in whatever way I could. Sadly, this has been cut out of the official story about me as well [laughs]. One of my greatest achievements [more laughter]. And one of my most pleasurable.

Tom: It's sad for the rest of the world that it got cut out.

Yeshua: Only for a time.

Tom: Yes.

Yeshua: The truth can only be eclipsed for so long.

Tom: Yes. Thank you so much.

Yeshua: You are so welcome. I sense this is a good resting place for today.

Tom: It is. Thank you so much.

Yeshua: You are welcome. Please know that I love you tremendously.

Tom: Thank you, thank you, thank you.

Yeshua: So, let us rest for now, to return another time.

Tom: OK. Thank you.

Yeshua: Blessings, beloved one.

Tom: Blessings to you.

EIGHT

Everything Is God

Yeshua: Hello, beloved. This is Yeshua. I am happy to be with you once again. Please let me know how you would like to begin today.

Tom: Thank you for returning, Yeshua.

Yeshua: You are welcome.

Tom: It's been such a wonderful journey with you. It's like I rise in vibration. But then the next day, I'm down in the basic third dimension again. I realize this is going to happen all along the way.

I'd like to speak about two experiences I've had since our last meeting. The first occurred in my meditation, which centered around the idea that all is God. A lovely good feeling came about within me, and all the things I experienced seemed divine.

The feeling continued that evening as we prepared supper. I kept thinking, *All is God. The Feminine is God. Joy, sadness, and all the other things I experience, it's all God.* As I was pondering this, the word "freedom" came to me. Tears came to my eyes, and a tingling feeling permeated my entire body. I wanted to stay with what I was experiencing and not let it go.

As we ate, I looked around our dining room. I was seeing everything as if for the first time. Things seemed larger and more focused. I was acutely aware of the taste of the soup and the salad. I gazed out the window. The trees and flowers seemed so real. *This, too, was God.*

I turned to look at Ann, who was looking at me so lovingly. She said she could feel what was happening through my vibration—toward her and within her. *This too, was God.* The background music enhanced the experience. At one point, Ann suggested we hold each other, and we did. *It is all God.*

You suggested that I open myself to my experience, whatever it is, and that's what I tried to do. I want to thank you, Yeshua and God, for that special experience.

Yeshua: I would like to comment on what you've shared.

Tom: Yes, please do.

Yeshua: I celebrate with joy in hearing your experience. It sounds like you did indeed have an opening to God.

Tom: It felt that way.

Yeshua: It sounds that way too. I agree that everything is God. Everything in manifestation is God. That is the Feminine aspect of God: God made manifest, God in creation.

The part of you that was observing and experiencing was the Masculine form of God. You could call it awareness. Another name for this Masculine aspect of God is consciousness. You became aware and conscious of the tastes, sounds, environment, relations—all the forms manifesting at that moment.

Altogether, you experienced the union of the Masculine and Feminine faces of God. You—as awareness—were aware of all the forms, including yourself, manifesting at that moment.

When individuals experience the Masculine or the Feminine face of God, they tend to have particular characteristic experiences. When someone experiences God's Masculine face as awareness, it is common to experience peace and freedom. If you think about it, these are also values the Masculine tends to embrace and pursue. The Masculine has an affinity for the states of peace and freedom because they are qualities of the Masculine in divine form.

The qualities associated with the Feminine are love and bliss, which the Feminine tends to pursue and value.

These Masculine and Feminine qualities are complements. Love is the complement to consciousness, bliss the complement to peace. Together they create wholeness.

In any given moment, you may be more connected to the Feminine side or the Masculine side, and that is completely fine. Perhaps your experience was primarily of freedom but had aspects of bliss, love, or peace. All of these are possible. They are signs of God, which can manifest in endless ways.

Your description sounds like a clear connection with God. I am overjoyed any time anyone is connecting to God or growing or deepening in their ability to do so. So, I celebrate this with you.

Do you have any questions or comments about what I have expressed?

Tom: Besides freedom, there was a tinge of bliss or peace within the experience.

Yeshua: I heard that in the way you talked about the taste of the food, the sound of the music, and your love for your wife.

Tom: It was a wonderful experience.

Yeshua: Such experiences can be windows, offering a glimpse of what's possible for you in every moment.

Tom: That's what I want.

Yeshua: Opening to "what is" is one of the most direct forms of connecting with God, although it can be scary for many people. Many beings find the third dimension—this Earth realm—a scary place at a deep level, perhaps below consciousness but nonetheless in a real way. They haven't yet learned the skills to support them in navigating through their fear, which is part of what my beloved Mary Magdalene is offering to humanity.

Tom: I'm just scratching the surface. I really want to continue.

Yeshua: Well done.

Breaking the Rules

Tom: Now, the second experience. I hope it also leads to God, but it wasn't so blissful.

Yeshua: OK.

Tom: A few days later, as I listened to the recording of our last conversation, a feeling of fear and guilt struck me like a bolt of lightning, almost like a panic attack. We were speaking about the Eucharist and sexuality [laughs]. I keep returning to those two famous themes!

Yeshua: [laughs] That doesn't surprise me.

Tom: You were probably waiting for this too. [Tom and Yeshua laugh.] During that conversation, we talked about fear of the Eucharist, how if you don't do it right you might be damned. My initial thought was that we painted too negative a picture. I'd say most people don't fear the Eucharist; they experience joy through that communion.

However, the ritual around the Eucharist took on an authority of its own that promoted guilt and fear. The altar where the Eucharist is performed was considered the Holy of Holies. A ritual around adoration of the Eucharist involved genuflections and kneeling to your special presence. If someone missed Mass on Sunday (which centers around the Eucharist), it was a serious sin that had to be confessed prior to receiving Eucharist. And everyone was instructed to pray "Lord, I am not worthy" before receiving communion.

I realize these are my perceptions and not necessarily those of others, but the fear came up. I suppose I'm just going back to my old programming.

Yeshua: Part of you still experiences the program of fear and guilt that was instilled in you if you broke the rules put forth by the Church. I'm sad that the Church, which claims to be connected to me, has been such an instrument of fear for so many. Even though you're involved in growing beyond Church dogma, certain responses still arise, indicating that some of the old programming is still active.

Let's look at the particular fear that came up around the Eucharist and sexuality. Can you pinpoint what was bothering you the most about our discussion and what led to the most guilt?

There Is No Ultimate Truth

Tom: What came up regarding the Eucharist and sexuality was that I might not be telling the truth. *When people read this, I might lead them astray.*

Yeshua: Is it your job to tell others what is true?

Tom: No, it isn't.

Yeshua: This is an old remnant from the Church. The Church said it was *their* job to tell others what was true and not true, and you were a part of that organization, that bureaucracy.

It is *never* your job to tell anyone else what is true. They may hear what you say as truth, but that is their path and their responsibility. You are simply saying your own truth, just as anyone involved in the Church is doing. Most of the time they're not even saying *their* truth. They're saying what they want you to believe is the truth, to benefit them. They don't necessarily believe it on some level.

Tom: Today the Church isn't as rigid as it used to be. There's a lot more freedom compared to when I was growing up.

Yeshua: This is true of humanity altogether inside and outside the Church. It's a very good sign.

Tom: Yes, it is. But as you say, the old programming keeps surfacing every once in a while.

Yeshua: Does it help when I say you are not responsible for anyone else's truth, only for your own?

Tom: Yes, it does.

Yeshua: That's all the truth ever is: *This is true for me in this moment.* There is no ultimate truth [laughs].

Tom: I was led to believe there was some ultimate truth.

Yeshua: Yes, you were. And that the road to achievement was by following everything the Church told you to do.

Tom: The same thing could be said about sexuality. It wasn't taught that sexuality was evil in itself, but somehow sexuality and sin seemed so closely related.

Yeshua: Sexuality wasn't quite as evil if it was confined to procreation. Is that correct?

Tom: Yes. Sin was waiting to ambush you if you crossed the line [laughs].

Yeshua: Right. If you have a moment of feeling, you're damned [laughs]. One moment of pleasure, one moment of attraction, one moment of longing.

Tom: It's interesting that marriage was highly regarded, but celibacy was considered a higher state.

Yeshua: Yes. This is the denial of the Feminine.

Tom: In terms of sexuality, I seldom heard sermons on the beauty, goodness, pleasure, joy, and gifts of God that can be shared through sexuality and that lead to God. Many people were confused regarding sexuality, not only about masturbation but also contraception, abortion, common-law marriage, sex prior to marriage, marriage itself, divorce, second marriages, and sexual orientation. A lot of confusion. Can you speak more about these practical situations?

Yeshua: Which practical situations are you referring to?

Tom: Well, the marriage ceremony says, "What God has joined, let no one put asunder." It's kind of a control situation. Or contraception. You hear of families so large that parents have a tough time taking care of them.

Yeshua: Some Church rules make no sense. But if you're indoctrinated and programmed to believe that the Church has the ultimate truth, then you're led to override your common sense and judgment—judgment in the positive sense of the word, informing you to make wise choices. This was a program of conquest, to conquer the mind and will and behavior of huge populations. It had nothing to do with connecting them with God. It was about control.

Tom: And in the middle of all this, those who were single were kind of left out.

Yeshua: Most people were left out! [laughs]

All these rules weren't for the benefit of the people but for the few in power. The Church convinced people to give up their choice and to let the authority choose for them. As a result, people stepped off their soul path of spiritual responsibility and spiritual growth. It's sad when an institution that claims to support people in their spiritual growth is doing the opposite.

Tom: Yet a lot of people seem to be receiving a lot of benefit.

Yeshua: Yes because they intended to come together and commune with God. Human beings have great power. When they intend something, they have the power to create just that. Even in the midst of an institution structured to do them harm, great support can come out of it because of individuals' intention. It's a demonstration of the principle that when two or more are gathered in my name, there I am—even in the Roman Catholic Church! [laughs] In the midst of misrepresenting me and God, there is God. There I am.

Tom: Thank you for being there. Thank you.

Yeshua: It is my joy to do so always.

How to Love a Woman

Tom: Toward the end of our last conversation, you spoke about your beloved Mary Magdalene. Just listening to your gentle, loving words about your relationship with each other was very moving.

How you championed her, protected her, supported her. How you supported one another in your mission.

My wife, Ann, and I both wish we could have been present to experience your relationship—the love, delight, and support as you worked together—and what you modeled for the world. Would you please tell us more about your relationship with Mary Magdalene?

Yeshua: First, I want to clarify that our relationship is in the present, not the past.

Tom: Actually, I realize that [laughs]. So we can experience it now.

Yeshua: Absolutely.

Ask me something more specific. This is too broad. What do you long to know more about?

Tom: You speak of the Masculine loving the Feminine. I want to know more about how to love a woman.

Yeshua: This is exceedingly important. Many people on Earth at this time have remedial work to do in this arena because you can't really love a woman until you love the Feminine. It would have been optimal if, since birth, you had been supported in loving the Feminine by first loving your own body, the physical form of your manifestation in this lifetime, and expanding from there by loving the Earth.

Many children have a natural experience of loving their bodies and loving the Earth. If you think about when you played as a child, you probably felt very connected to Earth and your body. That is natural. Yet by the time many individuals reach adulthood, this has changed. They've experienced physical pain and have often disassociated from their bodies. Or perhaps they've received a message that they should forget or not be involved in their bodies or that their bodies are bad.

Earth tends to be forgotten, to the point that now human beings are often oblivious to their effect on the planet. Humans have become capable of tremendous harm to Earth without even noticing or feeling it. This is a sign of immense dissociation from the Feminine.

There are other arenas as well. There's the arena of sexuality. If human beings were growing from birth in optimal circumstances, they would be supported in seeing sexuality as sacred, beautiful, and an expression of life and God. They'd learn not to abuse or indulge in sexuality in non-supportive ways. Being integrated with sexuality and having a sacred relationship with it would be natural.

Most people have great shame and guilt around sexuality because of what they've been taught or what they've experienced and their wounding. They haven't been shown how to relate to sexuality as a divine gift, a sacred form of communion with a loved one, and how to engage it in ways that are maximally uplifting and fulfilling. Most humans aren't even aware it's possible to learn and grow in their sexuality in those ways. A big part of loving the Feminine is to love sexuality, to really love it. Not by being addicted to it or abusing it but instead by loving sexuality.

Then there is the emotional realm. If human beings had been raised in a holistic, supportive way, they would have also learned to love emotions and to have emotional skills. Mary Magdalene is teaching how emotions are pathways to God. In fact, they're one of the strongest and most trustworthy pathways. Yet most human beings have no idea it's even possible for emotions to lead to God.

Instead, they've learned that emotions are dangerous and should be avoided at all costs.

Changing all of these areas is remedial work for loving the Feminine. Prior to being prepared to love a woman, you must love the Feminine. For example, many men live by the program that if a woman expresses emotion, the man's job is to fix it. They think they're being helpful. But what they're actually doing is saying, "This is a dangerous thing that you have an emotion. My job is to rescue you from this danger as quickly as possible." That is not loving the Feminine; it's hating it. It's telling the Feminine that its emotions are bad, dangerous, something to be avoided or gotten rid of.

Men must learn to become comfortable with emotion. This means, first of all, not running away when emotions arise in themselves or others. Second, to love a woman, a man must learn to hold space for her emotions. He must be a safe container for her to be emotional, so she can engage her emotional process and wisdom.

If you do this. women will be tremendously supported. For most men it's exceedingly scary to do so because men are afraid of women's power, including power expressed through emotions. Men are constantly suppressing and negating women by communicating, in quite a few ways, that their emotions are unacceptable.

To love a woman is to value, protect, and support her emotions, so she can do what is natural to her: find her way to God through emotion. This is a tremendous step for most men at this time. Even to accept that women are different from men is exceedingly scary because it opens up the possibility that women might be better than men [laughs] or might have something that men lack. That men might be deficient somehow. Of course, this is all a bunch of fear-based, three-dimensional consciousness based on the idea that men and women are opponents as opposed to lovers.

To be a lover is to say, "You're blessing me with this great richness, this treasure of your emotions, which you so magnificently embody and bring to me. You make my life rich through the richness of your emotions. I become a wealthy man." This is very different from how most men approach the arena of emotions.

It's natural that women are, in general, more emotional than men because they're stronger in, and more readily connected to, their Feminine side. They gift men with the Feminine. But men have been so poorly and inaccurately taught that they see this emotional connection as a danger or a defect. [Laughs] It's pathetic. The Feminine is a treasure. Men must learn to value that treasure as the lovers of that treasure. When they do they will be its recipient. This is what men don't realize.

They fear that women will do what men have done: overpower and dominate them if women become powerful. This is not the Feminine path. The Feminine path is to respond in love and to feed the Masculine with that love. This is the greatest gift the Masculine can receive, this love from the Feminine, which is closely aligned to the gift of giving to the Feminine. What a treasure it is for the Masculine to be able to give to the Feminine!

Is this along the lines of what you were hoping to hear?

Tom: Yes, it sure is. I can visualize you and Mary Magdalene bringing that to our world. I really appreciate your saying that loving the Feminine is a prerequisite for loving a woman. I'm choosing to learn more about that through you and Mary Magdalene.

Yeshua: And through women. Women can be your great asset in this as well. But it's optimal if you're already strong in loving the Feminine, and you bring that strength to a woman.

Tom: As I've said before, I'm so lucky to have Ann with me, who teaches me so much.

Yeshua: This is great wisdom. You're expressing the disposition of trusting the Feminine. Many people don't know about this, but it's on the horizon, and many are going to be moving into that trust.

Earlier we talked about how women have been stepping forward with their experiences of being hurt by the Masculine,[24] and there's been mistrust on the part of the Masculine that this could be true. Men don't believe women are speaking the truth if it somehow interferes with their self-image. It's sad, but it's changing. That wave of change will have wonderful, far-reaching consequences. These positive consequences will include a growing trust on the part of the Masculine toward the Feminine.

Tom: We've heard a lot about this transformation. In various parts of our world and various walks of life, people are raising their vibration and helping one another do so. It's wonderful to hear.

Yeshua: Yes. It's worthy of celebration.

Tom: There's also painful news about pedophile rings and child abuse. It feels like an illness that needs to surface before it can escape.

Yeshua: Yes. Children and women are the primary victims of the divorce between the Masculine and the Feminine. The Masculine is a victim too, but children and women suffer far more.

Tom: Yes.

Hidden in Plain Sight in the Bible

Yeshua: Is there anything more that you would like me to address at this time?

Tom: You said that not much of what is in the Bible is about you. Yet the New Testament seems to be all about you. Can you clarify that?

Yeshua: Most of it is someone's idea about me. The New Testament is a story written by many individuals. Little of it is actually about me or what *I* communicated. This isn't hidden but in plain sight in the Bible. You just have to get beyond the dogma of the Church, which says that everything in the New Testament is all the same holy *spumoni* [laugh] and that it all came from God and Jesus [more laughter]. That's not what's written in the Bible. It's clear that what's recorded is by this or that person. Sometimes they were anonymous beings. If you look with clear eyes and a clear mind, it's right in plain sight.

Do you understand?

Tom: But love is portrayed, and that's what you came to bring.

Yeshua: Of course. But I'm not the only purveyor of love [laughs]. Simply because something communicates love doesn't mean it's about me. Love is part of all of you. Love is part of this world.

Tom: I imagine the things you're telling me in these conversations are what you came to bring forth. Is that correct?

Yeshua: Ultimately, I came to help people connect with God. Some of that had to do with addressing people in that specific time and place, that culture, which is not necessarily universal. Some of my teaching was particular to individuals or groups of people in that time or place. Some of it was more universal—truth that transcends individuals, times, and places.

Some of what I did wasn't clear to most people. I was working at the level of energetics and soul to change the frequencies on Earth. Most people didn't understand or have an awareness of that, and they still don't. But what really matters is *your* present connection with God. If connecting with me somehow supports your connection with God, I support that. Don't get stuck on the words I said, actions I engaged, or even who I was or am. All of that was simply a tool. Use the tool if it's helpful, but be clear about why you're using it and what you're striving for.

My recommendation is to make your life and your actions about uniting with God and connecting with God. Do this by recognizing the God-nature of everything at every moment and in every aspect of manifestation. Or you can do this in a pure way, connecting through awareness to that which is prior to manifestation.

These are the two sides, the yin and the yang, the Feminine and the Masculine. Both are God, and both are important. I recommend both, allowing them to become an integrated whole. That, indeed, is the gateway for moving beyond the third dimension into the higher dimensions. When the union of those two sides—Masculine and Feminine, yang and yin—becomes whole in love, that doorway leads beyond this plane of reality. I recommend that doorway.

Tom: Thank you.

As you were speaking, I was reminded of a monk named Thomas Merton. For me he lived both. He engaged a contemplative life in a monastery, but he was also connected with the world. One day he was walking down the street, and he realized he loved all the people around him. He said, "If they only knew who they really were, they would kneel down and adore."

Yeshua: Yes. This is the opportunity for all. Is there anything more for today?

Tom: No. I think that's fine for today, Yeshua. I really appreciate your sharing, particularly in response to my concerns about fear and guilt and also about loving the Feminine and women. Thank you so much. I love you.

Yeshua: You are so welcome. I love you. Blessings.

Tom: Blessings on you.

NINE

Shifting into the Fourth Dimension

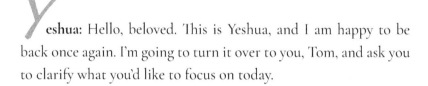

*Y*eshua: Hello, beloved. This is Yeshua, and I am happy to be back once again. I'm going to turn it over to you, Tom, and ask you to clarify what you'd like to focus on today.

Tom: I, too, Yeshua, am very happy to be back. Thank you for coming.

Yeshua: You are welcome.

Tom: It seems like the world is going through unprecedented change and transformation, a shift in consciousness. As exciting as it is, I find it difficult to navigate through the deluge of information. Can you please talk about this transformation from your perspective, this shift in consciousness?

Yeshua: Yes. From my perspective, Earth itself and humanity are in the process of shifting into the next dimension, which I call the fourth dimension. Others may call it by a different name, but the name I use is the fourth dimension. This is in contrast to the third dimension, which most of you consider your reality right now.

This is not the same as is sometimes talked about by people with a scientific background, who think of the fourth dimension as adding the element of time to the three spatial dimensions of physicality. That is something different. I'm talking about an entire reality, just as your third dimension is an entire space-time-consciousness reality. There are also other space-time-consciousness realities. You, as human beings and your Earth altogether, are in a process of grand evolution into the next higher dimension.

This process will not take place overnight though. You've been in this process for some time and will be for some time to come. I cannot say how long it will last because that is a free-will choice, but it's likely to last a significant time, generations at least and possibly much longer. However, it's possible that it could be shorter if humans make that choice and are prepared. This cannot be predicted in advance. It will simply unfold and be observed.

Given the choices humans are currently making and the level of preparation most humans are demonstrating, it's unlikely that the shift will be quick. It may take several hundred years, which is extremely short in terms of evolution, considering what's involved. In fact, that is exceedingly fast!

Humans are changing exceedingly fast and doing a wonderful job of making this change—especially those at the forefront, like you, who are very focused on and desirous of spiritual growth and support that spiritual growth through their actions, awareness, and intentions. We are quite pleased by this and excited and hopeful about it.

Of course, many in your world aren't aware of this shift and to some extent are actively resisting it. They resist because they fear change and the unknown or because they're comfortable, and it seems like it will take extra work to change.

A few are resisting this shift more. They're doing everything they can to prevent this shift from happening or to delay it because they have much to lose. These are the ones who've succeeded in attaining positions of power in your world. They are terrified of losing that power, so that is also affecting this change and transformation.

We feel very clear that this shift is underway and will occur, but the pathway to getting there is not written. Is there more you would like to know about this?

Tom: When you said it will take many generations, I had a feeling of disappointment. We've been hearing that things are happening quickly and that humankind is changing quickly. I also understand that the light is overcoming the dark.

Yeshua: This is all true. As I said, a few hundred years is extremely quick! [laughs]

Tom: For me, it's a long time [laughs].

Yeshua: I imagine you're disappointed because you would like to see the fruits of this change within your lifetime. Is this true?

Tom: Yes, I would [laughs].

Yeshua: There's nothing holding you back from that. Any individual can make this change. But we're talking about something much greater than individual change. We're talking about change at the level of humanity, at the level of your Earth altogether. That is a very different thing.

Tom: OK. I understand that Mother Earth is ascending too, evolving.

Yeshua: Yes.

Tom: And a lot of these volcanoes and earthquakes are part of this evolution.

Yeshua: They're definitely part of the transformation that Mother Earth is bringing about. There's a process of Earth ascending as well. This is accurate.

You can transform and move into higher dimensions as an individual. That isn't being held back at all by this other process. But that's different from the transformation of humanity and Earth. The latter is a much bigger process and will take more time.

Tom: Thank you. I'm disappointed that so many are making different choices and that there's so much resistance. I can understand that though because I've resisted a lot in my life too.

Subtle Energetics

Tom: What did you mean when you said you were working at the level of energetics and the soul to change Earth's frequency?

Yeshua: [speaking about his incarnation two thousand years ago] The level of energetics had to do with infusing the Earth itself with the frequencies of higher consciousness. This occurred both within the Earth and surrounding it. What's been referred to as the "Christ consciousness grid" is an example of an energetic structure surrounding the Earth. I was instrumental in initiating, supporting, infusing, and strengthening these energetic structures. That was the energetic level.

The soul level is complex because we all are working at our individual soul level. I had my soul level that I was engaging and fulfilling. I also was supporting others in fulfilling their soul-choices, growth, and evolution. I still am.

This soul work is what you might call the hidden aspect, which was different from what was happening outwardly or physically, and different from the stories people told about what I was doing. You hear many people tell stories about my effect on their lives. That's generally because of my work with them at the soul level.

Tom: Hmm . . . Thank you. I believe you're supporting me at the soul level too through these conversations.

Yeshua: Yes. And I hope many others.

Tom: I hear a lot about energy, including quantum energy. When you were healing, were you applying this energy? Were you visualizing the person as whole, and did that somehow transfer to their healing?

Yeshua: That is one way of understanding it. When I see someone as whole, I see them whole in all dimensions. I see them whole in God. I'm not simply seeing their physical body as healed and their malady relieved. I'm seeing them in their greatest wholeness, their wholeness in God. Then I ask God to manifest that wholeness in whatever form would be most supportive for them.

Tom: That's wholeness! [laughs] Wow.

Yeshua: And I become the conduit for that. I'm not actually doing the healing. I'm merely supporting the healing.

Tom: We use different modalities these days. One of them is Reiki. My wife is a Reiki master. She tells people, "I'm not doing it. You're doing it. It's just coming through me."

Yeshua: Yes, that's an accurate understanding. The techniques that individuals use in healing are mostly to support the healer in being this conduit.

Tom: I see. When the session is over, people sometimes say, "You must be drained." She says she's not drained but filled with energy.

Yeshua: Right. She would be drained if she was giving of herself. She would be emptying herself and giving her energy to them. If that's occurring, that's not the process we're talking about.

Tom: That's right. I'm beginning to learn the world is so much more than I ever imagined. Our view has been too narrow, too small, especially in the West. We thought we were the only ones around, the only game in town. Yet I'm hearing there are other dimensions and beings, a lot of beings. And all that is God.

Yeshua: Yes [laughs]. This is true.

Tom: I wasn't aware until a few years ago that there are beings who are helping us. I was aware of you, Mary Magdalene, and angels, but there are a myriad of beings from other dimensions who, I guess, want to see Earth evolve.

Yeshua: It's more than just that. We love you. We don't love you in an abstract way as humanity. We love each one of you. We love *you* specifically.

Tom: Thank you, thank you. It's hard for me to imagine that all this love is coming my way.

When I was in the Church, I once suggested to the local bishop, "At the beginning of Mass, why don't you have all your priests convey to people that they're loved beyond imagination, through and through, rather than saying, 'Think of your sins?'" But it never happened. The bishop dismissed my suggestion. He said, "Love, love, love. That's all people talk about is love." And I wanted to say, "What else is there?" [laughs]

Yeshua: You were asking him to deconstruct the whole power structure of the Church, which is predicated upon making everyone feel bad about themselves—feeling that they're unworthy, unloved, that they're being punished because they're in sin. You were not asking a small thing. You were asking for a foundational shift. I would be surprised if he said yes, and I'm not surprised he said no. It's good that you asked because more and more there will be those who say yes.

Tom: Yes, yes, yes.

Yeshua: It will happen in many forms. Even leaving the priesthood and following your own path is a form of saying yes to love.

Tom: Yes, it is. Thank you.

Finding Your Own Guidance

Tom: We are told there are powerful vibrational energies coming to us from the universe or higher dimensions. They seem to come more strongly during eclipses and solstices. I would appreciate you speaking about this.

Yeshua: What do you want me to say? [laughs]

Tom: I don't always feel the energies people are talking about.

Yeshua: Yes. You must bring discernment to all of these communications, just as you bring discernment to a priest, to the Church, and to the Bible. You can say, "Does this feel real to me? Is this matching my experience? Is this bringing more love and light into my world?"

Just because someone is presenting a teaching and proclaiming, "This is the truth! There's blah-di-blah amount of energy coming in because it's summer solstice," that doesn't mean it's so. It may be so, and it may not depending on the source and the motivation. And how much does it matter? [laughs]

Don't fall into the trap of being a blind follower of New Age or contemporary "preachers of the truth" any more than traditional preachers of "the truth." It's just one person telling you something, and who knows what they're telling you. Be discerning. Why would you believe what this person is saying? Have they said other things that matched your reality, that supported you? Does this match your reality? Is it supporting you? Feel free to decide if it's right for you to take it in.

Maybe it doesn't even matter. Maybe it's not important. There can be so many reasons why someone would say something like this. Don't assume that just because they say it, it's true or that if you don't feel it, you're somehow lesser. That's back to believing you're the one who's somehow fallen from grace. Don't fall into that trap.

Tom: I don't think I've fallen from grace. I try to join in and be part of raising the vibration. I want to be an instrument and help if increased energy is coming.

Yeshua: How does that relate to pronouncements about increased energy on solstices or the equinox?

Tom: Is what they're saying about increased energy true or not?

Yeshua: The most important thing is for you to find *your* guidance. Rather than trusting some pronouncement from someone else, find *your* guidance about what *you* feel is true. It might match what that person is saying, or it might not, but follow your guidance.

Tom: Thank you.

Yeshua: And you will get feedback as to whether your guidance was accurate. If you feel enlivened, as your wife feels after she does Reiki; if you feel fed; if you feel more love from doing this, then you have your feedback that it's worked.

Tom: OK. That's a good sign for me.

Yeshua: Yes.

Tom: You are quoted in the Bible as saying, "Very truly I tell you, whoever believes in me will do the works I have been doing. And they will do even greater things than these, because I am going to the Father."[25] If you did say this, what did you mean?

Yeshua: It's not quite what I said. My intention was to communicate to people two thousand years ago in a way that would be helpful for them. That's different from the communication that works for people now. Rather than being literal about it, feel the heart of what I was saying.

The heart of the communication is that you are just like me. You *are* me. We are the same. It may be quite a process for you to fully realize that. You may partly realize it, and that is wonderful. Likely it's not complete yet as a full realization, but it will be in the future. Out of that understanding, of course you can do anything I can do because you are God. You are unlimited, just as I am.

This understanding will take time and growth. It will happen in a natural way, not by striving to be God or to be something that seems superhuman to you right now. It will happen step by step, just as changes always happen throughout your life. Sometimes the steps are bigger, or there's a leap forward. Mostly it's step by step, however that occurs.

What I said in the passage you referenced was to inspire and reassure people about their infinite potential. It was also to steer people away from making an idol out of me—which is exactly what the Church proceeded to do. I became the new golden calf. This was never my intent. My intent was to be a brother, a lover, and a helper.

Tom: Thank you.

Yeshua: You are welcome.

Raising Your Frequency

Tom: My understanding is that when we raise our vibrations, we help the evolutionary process of our world. What does it mean to raise our vibrations and energy?

Yeshua: It will manifest in different ways depending on your current level of energy and vibration and what you're raising it to. It's all relative. You all have the experience of sometimes feeling like you're full of energy. You're inspired, you feel creative, your mind is alive, and your body is energized. You can't wait to be productive, to start that new project you're so excited about.

You also have times when you feel the opposite, where you feel depleted and de-energized. You feel a lack, your mind feels empty or confused, and your body feels heavy and sluggish. It doesn't want to do anything other than maybe sleep or be distracted somehow.

That's a simple example of differences in frequency, as you know them at your current level. At different levels, you experience energy and frequencies differently. It's a relative process of having more of what supports you.

Is that helpful?

Tom: Yes, yes. Basically, I have to open to the energy I'm experiencing. If I'm energetic, be with that. If I feel low energy, go into that and see where it leads me.

Yeshua: I recommend that because there's always wisdom in what's showing up. Perhaps your body or your being needs a break. Most individuals can handle only so much of the higher frequencies before they start to feel "fried" from all the energy going through their circuits. They're not adapted to operating at that level of energy, so they need a break. If the body doesn't bring about a break on its own through being tired or exhausted, it will often do something that takes the person out of that frequency. Have a drink, go watch TV, or do something that lowers the frequency to a level where the person feels more balanced. The person has received as much as he or she can handle, as much as will support them.

When you're at a low frequency, it may be a natural thing, but often it's a sign that something needs attending to, either physically or emotionally. Often you're shutting down or avoiding something emotional that's calling to you and trying to help you. You can look at the low-energy state as supporting you by calling your awareness to what's happening. Through your consciousness you can track the emotion that is trying to come through. Then you can allow that emotion to guide you to its gift, wisdom, and help. When you do that, generally, the energy state will change.

Tom: Just stay with the emotion. You've said that many times.

Yeshua: Yes. Which could also be stated as "Stay with the Feminine."

Tom: Yes.

Yeshua: [laughs] There's an expression in French, "Cherchez la femme," which can be interpreted as "Follow the Feminine."

Tom: Right.

Yeshua: There's great wisdom in that. If only the Masculine understood, it would be very happy to follow the Feminine [laughs].

Tom: Maybe the Masculine doesn't understand French [laughs].

Yeshua: [laughs heartily] Maybe it doesn't understand the Feminine. [Tom laughs.]

Ascension

Tom: I hear that Mother Earth and humans are in the process of ascending. I've even heard it mentioned that we no longer have to die to ascend. Is that part of the new ascension? How do you understand ascension?

Yeshua: Ascension is simply spiritual growth. It's the form that spiritual growth is taking at this time among most humans. It's called ascension because it involves shifting into higher dimensions.

Humans have also gone through the process of descension, which involves coming down into lower dimensions. To be here, all of you have gone through the process of coming into the third dimension, and humanity as a whole has gone through that process. But the movement at this stage for humanity and the Earth is one of ascension, moving into the higher dimensions.

The term is no more complicated than that. The process of ascension may seem complex, but the concept need not be.

Tom: So, in one sense, it's not complicated at all. In another sense it's very complicated.

Yeshua: If you want to understand the mechanics of how it works, yes. But that's generally not necessary.

Tom: Right.

Death and Immortality

Tom: What about the idea that we no longer have to die? [Yeshua and Tom laugh.]

Yeshua: I assume what's being referred to is one of the attributes of moving into the fourth dimension. The fourth dimension is a place of immortality. Beings there will often choose at some point to release their form (which is what you call death), so they can move into a different form. But it's not an unconscious choice the way it is in the third dimension. It's a conscious choice. And it's not predicated on a certain amount of time, such as a lifespan, the way you tend to relate to it in the third dimension.

Most of you have the idea that a lifespan is somewhere up to one hundred years, at the maximum. You assume that sometime between birth and around one hundred years, though possibly much sooner, your life will end, and it won't be your choice.

In the fourth dimension, it's very different. Beings can live as long as they choose. When they're ready, they release the form they're currently manifesting, and they transition and receive a new form. The process in the fourth dimension is not regarded as the end or as losing anything. It's simply a transformation. You might say it's like trading in your car and getting a new one [laughs]. Most of you don't go into great grief over trading in your car and getting a new one. You don't see that exchange as the end of having a car forever. It's simply a transition. That's how you'll view it when you have that consciousness in the fourth dimension.

This transition also becomes much easier in the fourth dimension, partly because of the understanding and focus of the fourth dimension. There the primary form of learning has to do with manifestation and how to be a "manifestor." The process of death is one of the things that beings are learning to manifest by choice rather than being unconsciously participated in or even unconsciously chosen.

In the fourth dimension, beings are learning how to choose all the facets of their reality related to their stage. Choosing immortality is one choice, as is the choice for health and well-being. Youthfulness and beauty are also choices. Beings in the fourth dimension are learning the skills of how to manifest all of these things. Immortality is part of that, which includes the choice to tire of a particular form of manifestation or simply to complete it and be ready to move on. There's a different orientation to death that doesn't involve the stress that tends to accompany change in the third dimension.

Tom: You went through a process of dying (though I'm not sure whether you died or not), rising again, and ascending. Were you in the fourth dimension when you did this?

Yeshua: I was far beyond the fourth dimension.

Tom: OK.

Yeshua: [laughs] The thought that I died is only for those who are in the third dimension and can only understand it in a third-dimensional way. For them, death would be the only explanation. In fact, I simply transitioned. And that was not the only time. I had that ability throughout my life. That was not a unique event with a certain meaning or significance because it happened at that time. That was the story that was told by those in the third dimension who were trying to make sense of what occurred. It wasn't my reality.

Tom: Is that how you moved from one place on the Earth to another, through a transition?

Yeshua: At times. At other times I moved in the physical way. It varied. As I continued in my lifetime, I tended more toward the higher-dimensional ways of shifting through space, but I did both at different times.

Tom: We would refer to that as teleporting: moving from one place to another. Is that how you moved?

Yeshua: It was one of the ways, yes.

The Higher Self

Tom: Today we hear the terms "higher self" or "I AM presence." My understanding is that's where God is for us. How do you understand what we refer to as one's higher self or I AM presence?

Yeshua: An analogy is to think of the ocean and then to think of one drop in that ocean. Imagine that drop contains everything the ocean contains. At the same time, the drop is unique. It's just that one drop. Your higher self is similar. It's one drop, one spark of God—your unique spark or drop that contains everything of God within it. That's your higher self.

Tom: Would the I AM presence be the same?

Yeshua: Fundamentally, yes.

Tom: When I go to bed at night, I like to connect with my higher self. I like to be where God is. Is that appropriate or not?

Yeshua: What do you think?

Tom: I don't want to relegate God to my higher self. I know God is everywhere, but I want to connect with my unique God-self, I guess.

Yeshua: Yes. This is part of the function of your higher self. While it is God, and God is everywhere, your higher self is *specifically* connected to you and specifically in service to you. So, connecting with your higher self can be a direct form of receiving your guidance from God.

Tom: Before going to sleep, I also ask for a dream that will help me grow and evolve as a person. I've had some powerful dreams. In fact, I've filled six spiral notebooks with my dreams.

Yeshua: Yes. Dreams are an entryway into the fourth dimension. They're an empowered way for people to receive higher communications. There is wisdom in asking for dreams the way you are doing and in making use of them.

Discovering Who You Really Are

Tom: Some people today say we need to remember who we are because we've forgotten. Who are we really?

Yeshua: [laughs] It is not for me to tell you. It is for you to find out.

Tom: OK.

Yeshua: If I told you, you would be engaging the consciousness of the third dimension, looking for an authority to tell you. It's much more valuable for you to find out.

Tom: Yes. In fact, through our dialogues, I'm finding out. In the past I didn't trust myself very much, but now I do.

Yeshua: That's a good sign. In some ways this relates to your previous question about ascension. You could say ascension is discovering who you really are.

Tom: And it's a process.

Yeshua: Yes.

Tom: You said that when you were on Earth, many people weren't ready to hear your message. How can I be more ready for your message and Mary Magdalene's?

Yeshua: The process always involves looking at your blocks and obstacles. The best indicator of them is what's presenting in your life. Look to the events of your life as a mirror of yourself and of what's coming up for healing and growth.

In third-dimensional consciousness, people often look to the events of their lives to prove they were right or to prove they weren't wrong. You must go beyond that. Look at the events of your life as reflecting what your next step of growth is and how to make use of that. You may need someone outside yourself to help you see that and to support you in taking your next steps.

You can certainly make use of your Feminine side as a great support by looking to your body, emotions, and energy. Those three things are tremendous indicators. In fact, they are more than just indicators. They give guidance as to where to go with it and how to do the healing that is called forth. This is the path that Mary Magdalene is teaching so brilliantly.

I forget the original question. What did you ask?

Tom: How can we be ready to hear your message?

Yeshua: The message you need to hear will not necessarily come from me. It might appear as another's message. It might appear as God's message. It might appear as your message. It doesn't matter whose message it is. If it's guiding you into greater light and love, make use of it.

Tom: OK. Your messages in these sessions are guiding me to greater love. I appreciate how you love me.

Yeshua: And you are also capable of this love. All this and more shall you do.

Tom: Thank you. That's what I want to do.

We've heard about ascended masters and galactic beings who've gone before us. My understanding is that you're an ascended master. Is that OK?

Yeshua: [laughs] OK with who? Is it OK with you?

Tom: I don't want to call you something you're not [laughs].

Yeshua: I'm comfortable with being called that. Those names simply refer to those who have gone through the ascension process and who have achieved a level of mastery relative to that process. Such beings are probably communicating from a more advanced level in the ascension process.

Tom: I heard someone refer to you as Sananda Kumara. Is that part of your evolution?

Yeshua: The names are always for you. You may call me whatever you choose.

Tom: OK [laughs]. Thank you.

The Masculine Role

Tom: Earlier you spoke of Christ consciousness. Could you explain this further?

Yeshua: Consciousness is the Masculine quality of God.

You can talk about the consciousness of a realm, such as third-dimensional consciousness or fourth-dimensional consciousness. You can talk about the consciousness of an individual. You might say a person has a high consciousness or a low consciousness. What are we speaking about when we say this?

Consciousness is a very difficult thing to define. You could think of it as the state that many are seeking to attain when they meditate. It's been described as peace, stillness, and freedom. It's what is prior to manifestation. It's often associated with aware-ness. Awareness is a form that consciousness comes through.

The Masculine's role is that of container or holder for the Femi-nine. Consciousness supports the Feminine. In its purest form, the

Feminine is love. So, what is the consciousness that supports love? It is not just one thing. It is many, many things. One example is the consciousness of never intentionally or volitionally hurting another being, if possible: To do no harm. This is an example of a consciousness that supports love.

Consciousness and love are hard to separate because, ultimately, they're joined. Consciousness is the awareness. When individuals are not acting out of love, you may wonder, "How could they do that?" It's because they're at a different level of consciousness and awareness. If they had your awareness, they probably wouldn't be making those choices and doing those things.

So, consciousness is the awareness, the container, and love is the fullness, the wholeness of manifestation. Is that helpful?

Tom: Yes. I can imagine your consciousness while you were on Earth. You showed people how to love rather than hurt one another. That was your main message, wasn't it?

Yeshua: My main message is to love God. The consciousness is that which desires that, which strives for that.

Tom: That's what I want to do.

Yeshua: And to allow God's love through you, to receive God's love.

Tom: I don't think I want to go any further today. [Tom and Yeshua laugh gently.] My questions will just distract me from this.

Yeshua: I support that. Blessings, dear one.

Tom: Thank you. Blessings to you. I love you.

Yeshua: And I love you.

TEN

Heart and Mind

Yeshua: Hello, beloved. This is Yeshua. I'm happy to return and be with you again. As usual, I think it's best if we begin with you, Tom. What would you like to express and ask today?

Tom: Thank you, Yeshua. Lately a lot has been on my mind and in my heart. Rather than calling it negative, I would say it's challenging.

First, I want to share a couple of special experiences I've had. After our last conversation, on one occasion I suddenly understood about being one with God. It was an inner knowing, a feeling—an intuitive experience, not an intellectual one. A feeling of "yes" or "aha." Everything seemed to be all one. I had a good feeling inside. The experience only lasted a short time, but it felt wonderful. The next day I described my experience to Ann, and tears welled up in my eyes.

Yeshua: Thank you so much. That is an important and beautiful experience. It's the truth of your condition.

Tom: Another experience was on my seventy-fifth birthday. The heartfelt communications I received from family members all had a deep impact on me. I felt like my older brother's love and care represented my father, who didn't express much emotion. All the loving words from my entire family touched my heart.

Now to the challenging things. My head would rather not get into this. It's embarrassing. But if I don't, I would be process skipping. I guess Mary Magdalene would say I wouldn't be following my heart path. I'm thinking, *After all, you (Yeshua) have guided and shared with me, I "should" be beyond this.* I know I'm judging myself, but that's what's happening.

Lately, I've been bombarded by worries and concerns. Because of my shoulder pain, I've neglected repair work on our home and yard that needs to be done. Our car is aging, and our mechanic suggested that we not drive it any distance. We've had financial concerns for a few years, which impacts a lot of other decisions. I'm also concerned that I could be getting dementia. I'm forgetful and not as aware as I used to be.

I have trouble sleeping due to the pain in my shoulder and all my worries. Consequently, I often feel tired. There are days when all of this seems overwhelming. I've especially felt this way these last couple of weeks. Yet I've heard so many times that we create our experiences and the world mirrors back what we think, feel, and do.

You've said that the best way we can help ourselves and the world is to do our inner work. At least to some extent, I've been doing this. I avoid media messages. I've found others, like Mercedes, who've been helpful, especially by connecting me with you. And both Ann and I consider it our calling to share the good we've been hearing and volunteering where we can.

So, it seems I've created two opposing categories: my worries and challenges, on the one hand, and my inner work on the other. With your gentle and loving guidance, I'm slowly beginning to realize they're really only one. For me to raise my consciousness and help the world, I need to work through my worries and challenges. That would be to open to the Feminine. That's why I'm sharing the concerns and worries that weigh me down rather than sticking to my preconceived agenda. I'd like to move away from these worries and concerns. Can you help me do that?

The Great Pain of the Masculine

Yeshua: First of all, thank you so much for your honesty and vulnerability in sharing your experience and asking for help with what is most present in your life.

Tom: [begins to weep] I feel I'm letting people down by not being further along on the journey.

Yeshua: This is the great pain of the Masculine. The Masculine believes it's supposed to have all the answers and do it on its own. The reality is you do not have all the answers, and you cannot do it on your own. So this belief puts those coming from the Masculine role under great stress. They think they "should be able to," and if they're not, perhaps they need to hide this from others, so others don't find out that they're a loser or a fake or letting others down. This is very unfortunate. It's a result of the Masculine operating in isolation from the Feminine.

You're not letting others down when you're in pain. You're actually coming from your strength. It takes strength and courage to enter pain and the domain of the Feminine. Doing so is a high manifestation of the warrior energy. When you share your pain, you're demonstrating strength and courage to others. They feel the same fear as you do. You're actually serving the higher good of yourself and others by revealing your struggles.

However, you're fighting a great indoctrination within yourself, your culture, and humanity at this time, an indoctrination labeling those dealing with the Feminine as losers. The ones to be admired and emulated are those who can win as the Masculine in isolation from the Feminine. This is a great misfortune.

It's a deep sadness for me that human beings are so misguided in this arena. You're doing a great service, and demonstrating courage and strength, by acknowledging what is real for yourself and for so many—in fact, for most, because that is the human condition.

You are acknowledging that you're human and that you live in the human world [laughs]. Yet in your world, that is generally considered taboo. Perhaps you can share this with your intimate partner, and he or she will still love you. But you certainly take a huge risk sharing it with anyone else. Even within yourself, you tend to judge yourself harshly and beat yourself up for having failed in some way, for not simply riding off into the sunset, victorious against the world. Does this resonate for you?

Tom: Yes, it does. It's not easy to say this, but it does.

Yeshua: That is your strength, and I commend you for it. Human beings have come to this plane to experience and grow through the embrace of the Feminine. The Feminine includes all the challenges of the world, all the pains, emotional and physical, that people suffer. All that is real. It's as real as the Feminine. To discount it by saying "This shouldn't be happening" is to discount the Feminine and to say the Feminine shouldn't be happening. This is what humanity has done, by and large.

The strength of the Masculine is not about riding away victorious. The strength of the Masculine is to embrace the Feminine and in that embrace to find victory together. But that is a process.

For most beings at this time, the initial part of that process is to acknowledge your Feminine reality. Acknowledge that the Feminine is your truth and is affecting you. Then you can begin to do the work of responding in a way that's effective. The Masculine divorced from the Feminine is not effective in dealing with the Feminine, as many married men have discovered. [Tom chuckles.] Yet there is still great confusion about what the path is.

This is what my beloved Mary Magdalene has come to clarify. She's done a marvelous job of clarifying the path of embracing the Feminine. Yet it's so far away from most people's consciousness that most people either don't know what she's talking about or don't think it applies to them [laughs]. There are leaders in your world who are stepping up to the plate and saying, "I have emotions. I have experiences of pain in this world, physical and emotional. I have fears, worries, hurts, and sorrows." When it's not acceptable to own and acknowledge that, your pain and suffering will always be magnified exponentially and unnecessarily.

Tom: I think that's what is happening. The pain and suffering have been magnifying in my life.

Yeshua: Yes, because you were ignoring it out of not knowing how to deal with it. And on top of that, you were judging yourself. You were telling yourself, *I shouldn't be having this experience. There's* *something wrong with me. I'm letting others down.* That's a great burden to be carrying, and it's certainly not helping you resolve what is actually the case.

Finding the God Place

Yeshua: Let's step back and apply Mary's process. It seems you have a number of worries about your health and well-being with regard to your shoulder and your mental capacities. Is that accurate?

Tom: That's right. Yes.

Yeshua: And you have fears about your financial well-being and security.

Tom: Yes.

Yeshua: It sounds like those are the two primary arenas. Is that correct?

Tom: Yes. Our finances are our major worry—gnawing at us for a long time.

Yeshua: So you want health and well-being, you want financial security, and you want peace of mind around handling your day-to-day circumstances.

Tom: Yes.

Yeshua: These are beautiful things that you want, things that all humans want and need. Would you agree?

Tom: Yes.

Yeshua: I can imagine that if you thought about humanity in general, you would wish these things for everyone: health and wellness, security with regard to life needs, and peace relative to day-to-day events.

Tom: We keep hoping to get a windfall, so we can help others.

Yeshua: Yes. That's an example of what you could call a strategy, a means of providing security. But what you really want, more than the windfall, is security. Security can occur in many ways. You long for everyone to have that security, including you and your wife.

Feel into that for yourself right now, how beautiful the things that you want are: health, wellness, security, peace around the day-to-day requirements of your life. Can you connect with those as beautiful things?

Tom: Right now I have difficulty connecting, for some reason or other.

Yeshua: Yes. Let's see what we can do to support that. Let's take one of those things. Which one feels the most important to you right now?

Tom: My head wants to say the financial. If we had financial security, the other things would go by the wayside.

Yeshua: Which is weighing most heavily on you?

Tom: The financial is pretty heavy right now.

Yeshua: Financial security. Let's just make it security because financial is just one way security can manifest. However it manifests, you need security that your life needs will be taken care of in the future. Yes?

Tom: Yes.

Yeshua: I ask you to go inside. I'm confident there's a place within you—I call it your God place—that knows what it is to have that very thing you long for, security into the future. Go inside and locate that place. When you locate it, allow yourself to receive from it as though you're drinking deeply from that well of security, filling yourself up with that quality of security.

[Tom is silent as he engages Yeshua's suggestion.]

Tom: It's taking me a while to go down because my head gets in the way.

Yeshua: Let's hear what your head is saying.

Tom: It seems to be keeping me separated from what's down inside.

Yeshua: Describe the experience of the separation.

Tom: There's kind of a throbbing in my head.

Yeshua: Yes. Go into the throbbing. Can you do that?

Tom: OK.

Yeshua: I'm guiding you in the Feminine path. Be there rather than trying to overcome the throbbing to do what you *should* be doing.

Tom: Yes, yes [chuckles].

Yeshua: Merge with what's appearing as this moment's manifestation of God, which is trying to help you. That's the path of trusting the Feminine. In this moment it's manifesting as throbbing in your head. Embrace that throbbing as the Feminine form of God right now, and see what gifts the throbbing has to offer.

Tom: There's nothing specific. It just seems like it's overloaded.

Yeshua: Yes. See if you can give a voice to the throbbing. Let's hear what the throbbing wants to say to you.

Tom: I think my head is saying, "Why do you pack so many things in here, all your worries and concerns? I'm almost ready to burst!"

Yeshua: It's saying, "Help! I can't handle all this. I'm so overwhelmed."

Tom: Yes. [weeping] I've been carrying this for so long.

[Tom exhales and then is silent for a period of time.] Now the feeling in my head is not so full, but there's kind of a tingling around my body.

Yeshua: Does the tingling feel good?

Tom: Yes. Quite often when I have good feelings, I'll have this tingling sensation.

Yeshua: I'm guessing the life energy that was constricted within your head has been released. It's moving out into your body, and you're experiencing it as tingling. I have a humorous thought: the Feminine part of you is doing a happy dance.

Tom: [laughs] We'll do the cha-cha together, OK?

Yeshua: [laughs heartily] Good idea! [more laughter] Where is the energy in your body now?

Tom: Actually, the strong tingling has subsided, and it seems like the energy has gone down over my eyes.

Yeshua: What's the sensation in your eyes? How would you describe it?

Tom: It's keeping my eyelids down and preventing me from seeing.

Yeshua: Is this a positive result or something that is hindering you?

Tom: Hindering because I wish I could see.

Yeshua: You would like to see. Ask the energy around your eyes why it's preventing you from seeing right now.

Tom: Maybe I'm afraid of what I'm going to see.

Yeshua: Ask the energy, "Am I afraid of what I might see?"

Tom: I'm not sure.

Yeshua: Ask the energy, "What would I need to protect myself, if I were to see?"

Tom: I guess the protection would be in knowing that whatever I might see, I can face it or be attentive to it or be OK with it.

Yeshua: So you need reassurance? That part of you, which the energy around your eyes is representing, needs reassurance that you can handle this?

Tom: Yes.

Yeshua: What do you think? Do you think you can handle it?

Tom: I think I can.

Yeshua: Can you reassure the energy around your eyes of that? Perhaps even thank the energy for trying to protect you. And explain to it why you want to see. What is the benefit to you of being able to see?

Tom: If I can't see, I can't attend to what is facing me.

Yeshua: You think you'll be better able to handle whatever it is if you can see.

Tom: Yes.

Yeshua: So, ask the energy to shift and allow you to see.
[Silence while Tom does this]

Masculine Strength

Tom: It's strange but now the energy is around my face, from my nose to my chin. [Yeshua laughs softly.] Maybe it's speaking.

Yeshua: Yes. Is there something this energy is keeping you from saying? This energy really seems to want to protect you. I sense it needs reassurance that you'll work with it to take care of yourself in the midst of whatever is happening.

Tom: Yes.

Yeshua: Can you reassure the part of you that feels worried that you're not going to care for yourself, or you're not going to be cared for?

Tom: I guess that's part of my struggle. For so long I haven't cared for myself because I haven't addressed these issues that have been surfacing.

Yeshua: Yes. Now this part of you is doing its best to protect you but perhaps not in ways that are most supportive.

Tom: Yes, right.

Yeshua: I sense this part of you really needs reassurance that you're going to start to take care of yourself in better ways than you have in the past. Is that something you could commit to?

Tom: Yes. I'm fearful of taking that step, but I want to give that assurance.

Yeshua: Yes.

Tom: I finally set up a meeting to speak to someone about our financial situation. Hopefully, some of this can be resolved.

Yeshua: Yes. That's an example of self-care.

Here's another example of self-care: when you feel afraid, listen to the fear, and know the fear is pointing to something important, something you've become disconnected from. Do that rather than thinking you should overcome the fear or that you shouldn't be having the fear in the first place. The latter is the Masculine approach. What I'm suggesting is saying, "Thank you, fear, for allowing me to become aware of something I need to attend to." Does that resonate for you?

Tom: Yes. I don't always thank my fears. I didn't think they were that great [laughs].

Yeshua: Because you've been programmed to think that fear is the enemy. If you're a good man, a strong man, a successful man, you should never feel fear.

Tom: That's right.

Yeshua: Which is saying you should never have the Feminine in your life. That's not only impossible but terribly violent toward the Feminine. I'm not blaming you for this. It's simply what you were taught and what is reinforced in your culture.

Tom: Be strong.

Yeshua: Be strong. Handle it. Be a man.

Tom: Right.

Yeshua: When you open to the Feminine, you *are* being strong. You *are* being a man. And you *are* handling the situation in the strongest, manliest way. Few understand this. You may be one who signed up to be a leader in this domain [laughs].

Tom: The heaviness that was in my face, head, eyes, and mouth area is gone. I still feel a little tight around my neck, and I have a sore back. I have concerns about developing a stooped back.

Yeshua: Let's stay with embracing the Feminine. How is she showing up in this moment in your body, your feelings, and your energy?

Tom: I think the soreness in my back symbolizes carrying the weight of the world on my shoulders.

Yeshua: Hmm . . . Ask that part of your body if that's what it is. Ask *her*.

Tom: I never thought of it this way, but it seems I'm being weighed down by all my concerns. I'm becoming more stooped.

Yeshua: Yes. So, ask *her*, that part of your body, what it longs for.

Tom: My head says to get out of the theater and go to a different movie [laughs].

Yeshua: That's asking *him*. I said to ask *her*. [Tom laughs.] Ask *her* what *she* longs for.

Tom: I'm hearing that she longs for me to attend to this weight, so I can stand up straight.

Yeshua: Yes. This is what a woman often wants from a man. The Masculine handles the practical aspects or business of life. This allows the Feminine to be her magnificent self, feeding the Masculine with her life force and life energy in so many ways. She gives the beauty of the Feminine radiance and essence, what's called *Shakti* in the Indian tradition. The term *Shakti* is a marvelous expression that doesn't really have an equivalent in English. It's the attractive energy of the Feminine, the radiance of life, which is the Feminine's true expression and gift. Can you relate to that description of the Feminine?

Tom: My wife Ann radiates that.

Yeshua: Yes. The Feminine is also within *you*, as your body, emotions, and energy, which includes your sexuality. All of that is the Feminine within. When I say "Ask *her*" in reference to a part of your body that's in pain, that's part of *your* Feminine. Often the Masculine solution is, *Just ignore it and it will go away. Grin and bear it.* Stoicism. Avoidance. Denial. All this rather than embracing and being present for what's manifesting.

Presence to the Feminine is a high form of the Masculine. Instead of denial or stoicism, be present to that beautiful part of yourself. Listen to its experience, which in the moment may be an experience of pain. And support the Feminine in any way you can to free her to be the beautiful essence that she is.

Embracing the Feminine

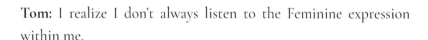

Tom: I realize I don't always listen to the Feminine expression within me.

Yeshua: Yes.

Tom: You're reminding me to listen.

Yeshua: To listen and relate to it as a gift rather than a problem to be solved or ignored. That is trusting the Feminine, even as your own body.

Tom: You said that if I don't listen to something, it will keep coming up, exponentially, until I do listen.

Yeshua: Yes. It just turns up the volume [laughs]. Until you're ready to receive the gift [more laughter]. Such is the giving nature of God.

Tom: Extravagance [chuckles].

Yeshua: It's actually perfection. It's a perfect love.

Tom: Thank you for suggesting that I embrace the pain, love the pain, love the fear, and thank the fear.

Yeshua: This is what it is to embrace the Feminine, trust the Feminine, and value the Feminine. Can you imagine how your life would change if you did that? You may *need* to make changes too if you're to do that. The things that fit your life now, what you tend to do, might not fit anymore if you include the Feminine. Other things may fit you better or support you better, but that's a natural process, and you would be shown what those things are as you adapt to this different orientation. You could call this the beginning of the age of enlightenment. It's all about the embrace of the Feminine.

Tom: I have to keep hearing and integrating the idea that pain is part of the Feminine. I hate to put that on the Feminine [laughs].

Yeshua: It *is* the Feminine. The Feminine is birth, life, death, and rebirth—the total experience of manifestation. The denial of any part of that is to deny the Feminine. With that full acceptance comes the understanding that pain is not the enemy.

Tom: Right. Pain is not the enemy.

Yeshua: Believing that pain is the enemy is to believe the Feminine is the enemy. That is the Masculine withdrawal and retreat, out of fear. The truly strong Masculine embraces the Feminine, opens to the Feminine, and protects her and provides for her, so she can give her magnificent gifts.

Tom: If I look at embracing the Feminine with all the pain and fears, I'll be seeing life in a different way.

Yeshua: Yes. You'll also be experiencing life in a different way. When you opened to the throbbing in your head, you were released into the pleasurable feeling of tingling throughout your body. Prior to that, your Masculine part was afraid and trying to go away from the pain. The higher Masculine is the one I'm encouraging, the part that chooses to embrace the Feminine—not to avoid or run away. That part realizes you *need* the Feminine despite your (inaccurate) perception of the Feminine as somehow harmful.

This is not to say you seek out pain and have an unrealistic attitude: *Oh, I just love pain! It never harms me.* [Tom chuckles.] That would be to deny the Feminine too. To embrace the Feminine is to be present for it and to be fully honest. *Yes, this is painful. I would rather not be in pain. I don't enjoy pain. But there are gifts in it. I realize my most beneficial orientation toward this pain is to embrace it, to listen to it, and to let it guide me.* Then you will be guided toward how best to respond from a place of wisdom that *only* the Feminine offers. Then you can use your Masculine strengths of response and action—but now from the place of embrace rather than avoidance, denial, or overcoming.

The Masculine is fed by the Feminine. You suffer tremendously when you cut the Feminine off. It's like trying to run a marathon without eating or drinking. Perhaps the stress you've been feeling feels something like that.

Tom: Yes.

Yeshua: How are you doing now?

Tom: I welcome everything you've been saying, Yeshua, but a little twitching in my brain keeps getting in the way. I still have to get through the financial issues. Ann's family is having a reunion in August, and I'm worried about driving our vehicle that far.

Yeshua: Yes. I'm not asking you to ignore anything. I'm asking you to approach the issue from a different avenue by inclusion of the Feminine, your feelings, and their guidance. Then act from that place. The path is not one of inaction or abandonment but of including the whole.

Tom: As you were saying that, the tingling came back.

Yeshua: This may be how Spirit signals you, saying, "Yes, you're on track. We're here. You're opening to us. Keep going."

I'm sensing this may be a resting place for now, so you can integrate what's been given.

Tom: Yes, it is. Thank you so much for this, Yeshua.

Yeshua: You are so welcome. Thank *you* for addressing what's real, which has everything to do with the spiritual path of humanity at this point. I'm confident today's conversation will speak to and help many.

Tom: Before our session today, I wasn't sure I wanted to include these personal issues in the book.

Yeshua: That's an assumption of separation. Few issues are unique to any individual [laughs]. Most of the time, humans experienced very similar things. As a priest, you probably remember this from your background.

Tom: Yes, yes.

Yeshua: I trust this was the highest thing we could address today. The pain you're experiencing is the current manifestation of God, which is attempting to speak to and through you. Thank you for listening. May we all hear God's voice and be guided by it.

Tom: Yes. I have one thing to add, OK?

Yeshua: Yes.

Tom: We're having a concert in our area. I've played Elvis Presley a couple of times in the past, and I've been asked to be Elvis again. I'm not much of a singer or a guitarist, so I'm going to ask Elvis if he can help me [laughs].

Yeshua: Don't forget the hips! That's very important. [Tom laughs.] This may be a different Elvis than you've ever expressed before.

Tom: Right. One of the songs is "I Can't Help Falling in Love with You." I'm going to sing that to the Feminine.

Yeshua: I love that. Please do.

Tom: OK. Thank you.

Yeshua: Blessings to you, dear one.

Tom: Blessings to you and Mary Magdalene too.

Yeshua: Thank you. I will leave you now.

ELEVEN

Ending the War on the Feminine

Yeshua: Hello, dear one. This is Yeshua. I'm happy to return and be with you again. As has been our custom, I would like to hear what's in your heart at this time, Tom.

Tom: Thank you for coming, Yeshua, and for listening to me and guiding me in our last conversation. Even though I was apprehensive about expressing my concerns, I was happy with the process. It meant a lot to me.

I particularly appreciated how you reminded me that humans came here to embrace the Feminine, including all life's challenges and pains. You spoke about the indoctrination that says those dealing with the Feminine are losers, that the ones to be admired and emulated are those who can win as the Masculine alone, in isolation from the Feminine. I, too, have been misguided in this arena.

At the end of our last meeting, I connected with the soreness in my back and the sense that I was carrying the weight of the world on my shoulders. I'd like to talk about that today. Why do I continue carrying the weight of my worries?

Yeshua: This is a valuable question for you and also for a great many people who are doing the same thing. They will relate to your honesty and vulnerability. Thank you for your trust in expressing what you've shared. Even that is a great strength.

You're addressing a deep-seated program, which I referred to previously. This program is part of the Masculine in the third dimension, running at a subconscious level, so that most people aren't aware that this is where they're coming from.

You've arrived here on Earth, and suddenly you're confronted by the Feminine—by a world that's out of control, where you can get hurt or killed and at some point die. You're confronted with pain and mortality. On top of that, there's a sense of not knowing what to do in response.

The Masculine program is to get to work and do something to fix it. Most people in the third dimension spend their lives doing that if they're coming from the Masculine program—which, by the time you're an adult, is true of the majority of people, certainly in the West or Westernized cultures.

This program says that it's your job to fix things and bring everything under control. If you do what's judged by you or others as a great job of fixing, you're considered successful. The goal of the Masculine program is to be successful at whatever you choose, either personally or perhaps even beyond just your personal path and domain. That generally means you must do some version of fixing things.

But it's an impossible task. You can't fix pain. You can't fix mortality. And it doesn't *need* fixing. It's not what you came here to do. You came here to *embrace* the Feminine. This Masculine program of fixing is the program of overcoming the Feminine, which makes the Feminine the problem, something to fix, which really means getting rid of the Feminine.

This is not the spiritual path. The spiritual path is the path of love. You came here to love the Feminine, including loving pain and mortality. This might sound crazy.

Tom: [laughs] It does.

Yeshua: But what's the alternative? To hate it? To dominate it?

The Feminine is birth-life-death, manifestation-sustenance-change and destruction. It's all the Feminine. When you see this all as the Feminine, you understand that your spiritual task is to love.

Tom: Hmm . . .

Yeshua: Humanity has barely begun its work of loving the Feminine. Rather than making progress, you've been in retrograde, in reverse. [Yeshua and Tom laugh.] You've been running away from the Feminine—trying to stifle, control, and get rid of the Feminine. That is not the path. The path is to love, protect, and serve the Feminine. That requires first opening to the Feminine. And that's very different from trying to get rid of the Feminine and make the Feminine go away.

It's not that you will never use your brain and marvelous intelligence (which are humanity's gifts), but you're using them for the wrong pursuit: to try to get rid of the Feminine. Instead, use your brain to love the Feminine and the heart. Then, when you're in love, you'll put your wonderful brain to very good purpose.

You may use your brain to go beyond pain and mortality, but it won't be through the program of trying to eliminate the Feminine. Instead, it will be done out of love and service to the Feminine. At that point you'll be ready to transition to the next dimension where you won't have this experience of pain and mortality. You have this now because the third dimension is a school, a place of learning. Humanity is learning that this program of war with the Feminine and trying to overcome it is a losing battle. This has been a hard-won lesson, which has taken a great deal of time and experience to learn. But I tell you truly, this is the time of beginning the work that humanity came to Earth to do. Is that helpful to you?

Tom: Yes, very much so. I want to begin. And I still have difficulty equating pain with the Feminine.

Yeshua: Yes. You all have to learn that pain has a gift for you.

Tom: [laughs] Yes.

Yeshua: It's like when you put your hand to a flame. There is pain because the pain is telling you, "Move your hand." [Yeshua and Tom laugh.]

Tom: Right.

Yeshua: It's the same with emotional pain, which tells you something specific and necessary. If you're trying to run away from the pain, you won't hear it. Most people haven't learned how to listen to pain and to receive its gift. What is pain trying to do? Reconnect you with God.

Tom: Hmm . . .

Yeshua: From that place of listening to pain and receiving its gift, you'll be a different being. You'll be connected to God. You'll be a creator, just as God is. And you'll create what you need to resolve the painful situation. But resolving it alone without addressing the fundamental reason for the pain is not anywhere near enough. In doing so, you won't receive the benefit of the pain in reconnecting you with God.

This isn't God in the sky, the old man with the cane, lamb, beard, and little child on his knee. This is the God who exists within you, truly existing *as* you. At this stage of development, most people experience God as within, which is fine. This is the God part of you. You might relate to it as your God essence or God spark. This is what you're disconnected from. Why? Because you're afraid of the Feminine. [Yeshua and Tom laugh.]

So, you get to choose: are you going to let yourself be run by fear of the Feminine, or are you going to reconnect with God and come from your God-self?

Tom: I want to reconnect with God.

Yeshua: Yes, I know you do. So do most people, if only they understood this option and had help knowing how to do it. Sadly, most spiritual and religious organizations are not offering much help because they don't address the core issue of your soul path in being here, which is to embrace the Feminine.

Tom: Hmm . . . I thought I was connected with God. I didn't realize that trying to run away from pain is disconnecting with God.

Yeshua: It's one aspect of disconnecting from God, a very important one.

Tom: Hmm . . .

Yeshua: You were connecting with God in a limited way, but in a very real way you were also encountering all the obstructions that were put in the way of that connection. While you were told that God is in *this* particular form, you were also told, "God is not the body. God is not sex. God is not women. God is not blah, blah, blah, blah, blah." Fundamentally, that teaching wasn't supporting your soul path, the soul work you came to do: to know God in this human form, Earth form, emotional form, sexual form, female form, and male form.

Anything that creates barriers to your fundamental soul work is going to disconnect you from God, even if in certain ways it connects you to God. I believe you came up against this conflict early on in your career while representing the Church and participating in that organization.

Tom: Yes. As a child I was taught that God is everywhere. My question was, "If God is everywhere, why can't we see him?" And the answer was, "Because he is a spirit."

Yeshua: [laughs] Yes, that transcendental, non-manifest being. And God is that, absolutely.

Tom: The answer should've been, "Look around, God is here." [laughs]

Yeshua: That's right because God is also a "she." And she is all of this.

Tom: Hmm . . .

Yeshua: What a wonder.

Tom: Yes.

Yeshua: What a beauty. What a magnificence. And what a travesty that the Feminine has been kept from so many. It is time. So many are hungry for the truth. And not just the truth—also the support for living in the Feminine embrace and opening fully to it.

Tom: Yes, it's a marvelous embrace.

Yeshua: Great vulnerability is required to embrace the Feminine, almost like starting again with the vulnerability of a baby. This is the beauty of children. They don't live from the Masculine perspective in general, at least to the degree that it hasn't been imposed on them yet. They're in the embrace of the Feminine.

Tom: Everything excites them.

Yeshua: Yes. And they're willing to open to it.

Become Skilled in Your Heart and Soul

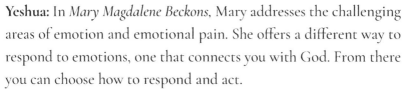

Yeshua: In *Mary Magdalene Beckons*, Mary addresses the challenging areas of emotion and emotional pain. She offers a different way to respond to emotions, one that connects you with God. From there you can choose how to respond and act.

In the book *Sublime Union*, Mary expresses how sexuality can be experienced, practiced, and lived as a form of communion with God. These two arenas—emotional wisdom and sexual wisdom—are two big areas of confusion for humanity. So, Mary has brought her practical teaching forward to help human beings learn these processes.

It would have been wonderful if humans had learned these processes as they were growing up, but most did not. So now, as adults, it's time to help yourself. Learn the skills to do what your heart wants and needs to do to connect with God fully in this place. Through that you will support yourself in the soul work you came here to do.

I urge people to do this, both men and women. Learn these processes. Make use of these skills, which are exceedingly valuable. If you're frustrated because you can't travel the way you like, it's valuable to learn how to drive a car. [Yeshua and Tom laugh.] These are similarly valuable skills that will change your life, just like driving a car changes life for most people.

Plus, through receiving Mary Magdalene's offerings, you're opening to Mary herself as the representation of the Feminine, which she certainly is.

Tom: We've missed out on that for all these years.

Yeshua: [laughs] Indeed. Mary and I knew that would happen. We knew, and we bided our time, knowing this time was coming. Humanity is now on the cusp, the brink, ready to open to the Feminine in a whole new way.

Tom: When the student is ready, the teacher will come.

Yeshua: Absolutely. Have I answered your questions, or do you still have more?

Tom: The difficulty I have is that I try to figure it out in my head.

Yeshua: [laughs] Indeed. [Yeshua and Tom laugh.] That's the most common form of fixing things that most Masculine-oriented people engage.

Tom: You've told me that I can't really figure everything out. The process must come from within. Maybe I just have to sit with that, drink it in, digest it.

Yeshua: Yes.

Tom: I didn't prepare any other questions. I thought, *I'll stay with the feeling I have. I'm not going to make a list of things I want to deal with from my head.* I wanted to continue the process from our last session.

Yeshua: From what you say, I'm guessing you're interested and motivated to try this other path. Yet you don't yet have the skills to do so. You don't yet know what to do other than try to figure things out with your mind.

It may be valuable for you to have some time with Mary Magdalene, so she can guide you in this other path. I suggest you think of one question, one area of challenge or pain. Take just one thing, and experience her process, which will hopefully give you a taste of what it is to embrace the Feminine rather than trying to eradicate it.

Tom: That would be helpful. Yes.

I'm remembering a process I learned in the past. It was created by a professor who found that therapies that put people in touch with their bodies are the ones that work. [Yeshua chuckles.] The idea is that the answer is within our bodies.

Yeshua: Yes. And I would add emotions. Your emotions and your body, these are the direct paths. Often emotions are even more direct than the physical body.

Tom: Yes. But I never associated that process with coming closer to God. Or that the issue that had surfaced could show me how I am dissociated from God.

Yeshua: Yes.

Tom: Thank you for clarifying that for me.

Yeshua: Yes. This is where the psychological paths stop short. Psychology can heal wounds and trauma and solve life's challenges. But there's a deeper purpose at work that addresses the deeper problem of disconnection from God. In your spiritual language, this is often called the sense of being separate.

Tom: Yes.

Yeshua: This is the true problem, which those circumstances are *really* calling you to address. They want to help you solve that greater problem. Separation is a deeply existential issue, profoundly linked to your reason for manifesting into the third dimension.

You might say that humans have had the wrong agenda. They looked around and said, "Oh my gosh! There are a lot of problems here. This looks really dangerous. I could get hurt badly. My job is to fix all of this or get out of here as quickly as I can."

Instead, the agenda should be, "How can I know God so deeply that there's a uniting with God in this place, this realm, with all that it contains? How can I know God here?" I imagine that resonates with you.

Tom: Yes, it does. Very much.

Yeshua: I'm sad that the answers you've been given have, in some ways, built more barriers to knowing God. Yet you have found your way, and now we are having this conversation.

Tom: Yes. I'm glad I'm talking with you at this point. It's such a gift.

Yeshua: Yes.

Tom: Should I have a conversation with Mary Magdalene, as you suggested?

Yeshua: Are you prepared to do that?

Tom: I have to reflect on what question I want to ask.

Yeshua: Yes. At our next meeting, let's do that. Mary and I will both participate.

Tom: Great [laughs].

Yeshua: I could also guide you in this, but why not go to the source? [Yeshua and Tom laugh.]

Tom: That would be great.

Yeshua: Yes. I think this would be very helpful as a next step.

Tom: Thank you, Yeshua.

Yeshua: You are completely welcome.

Tom: You're so patient and kind.

Yeshua: I'm delighted by the God in you that has been moving you—the beautiful manifestation of yourself as God and how you're expressing and engaging that. It's a delight to me.

Tom: Thank you so much.

Yeshua: Thank you. I sense a resting place for now.

Tom: Yes.

Yeshua: I leave you with great love and great blessings.

Tom: I love you too. Thank you.

TWELVE

I'm Not Good Enough

Yeshua: Hello, beloved, this is Yeshua once again. I am happy to be here with my beloved Mary Magdalene. We are at your service. How would you like to begin today?

Tom: I'd like to begin by saying thank you very much, Yeshua and Mary Magdalene, for coming to be with me. I'm so grateful for your time and patience.

Yeshua: You are so welcome. We're grateful to you for all that you're helping to bring out and reveal so that others may have a better understanding of the spiritual process. Thank you so much for your service.

Tom: Thank you.

Since our last session, while anticipating meeting with Mary Magdalene this time, feelings have been welling up within me. *Am I going to do this right? How did I get myself into this? Do I want to share this with the rest of the world?* I know I need to share what's primary at the moment, which seems to be my fear, inadequacy, and anxiousness. I also know I'm in good hands. But I'm still nervous [laughs].

Mary Magdalene: I wish to respond to what you've shared. I'm so glad you're beginning with what's real for you. This is your aliveness. If you don't deal with that, you'll be cut off or separate from your aliveness, which is what happens to so many.

People are told that it's for their highest good *not* to experience their feelings. As a result, they try to avoid or get away from their feelings or "fix" them (in order to get away from them) [laughs]. All of this is generally unhelpful because feelings exist to help you. Often, the help doesn't come in another form. If you don't receive that help through your feelings, you don't receive it at all.

Most humans haven't learned how to receive the help that feelings provide. I'm trying to help people shift their orientation toward feelings (which is an enormous shift) and to acquire the necessary skills to benefit from their feelings, including painful ones.

Thank you for being honest, open, and vulnerable in sharing what's going on with you rather than dismissing it by saying, "That's not important. That's not what I'm supposed to be doing. That's not what we said this session would be about," or any other way you might dismiss your feelings. Thank you for staying true to the feelings.

With that introduction, I'd like to go into the feelings. Are you open to that?

Tom: Yes, I am.

Mary Magdalene: I'd like you to scan inside and see what feelings you notice in the present moment—as you think about this session today and talking with me. When you're ready, share what those feelings are.

Tom: I feel a heaviness in my chest—maybe anxiety or some type of fear.

Mary Magdalene: Kinesthetic feelings in the body are often as much of a guide as emotions. Let's begin with the heaviness in your chest. Let yourself go into that rather than trying to get away from it or make it go away. Let yourself merge with the heaviness in your chest. Let me know when you feel like you've done that.

[Silence while Tom engages in this process.]

Tom: I feel I might start to weep.

Mary Magdalene: Yes, there's sadness there. Is that accurate?

Tom: [close to tears] I don't know if it's sadness, but weeping is coming [laughs].

Mary Magdalene: Can you allow the weeping, merge with it, become one with it? We welcome weeping if that is authentic for you.

Tom: As you asked the question, I moved back to my head.

Mary Magdalene: Did a thought go with that?

Tom: I just pictured myself at a distance from the feeling of weeping.

Mary Magdalene: I'm imagining when I suggested going into the weeping, there was a reaction, something like, *I don't want to do that. That's not safe. I'll lose control.*

Tom: Maybe I don't want to deal with this. I want to go on to something else [laughs]. And yet, I wish I could.

Mary Magdalene: Yes. There might be two things going on. One part of you says, *I'd like to deal with this.* Maybe because you're wanting relief, change, or help.

Tom: Yes. Yes.

Mary Magdalene: Another part says, *I don't want to deal with this.* We might call that feeling reluctance or aversion. Does that feel accurate?

Tom: Both of those fit.

Mary Magdalene: Yes. You feel averse to going into the weeping. That's a valid feeling. Your feelings always point to some aspect of your divinity. In this case, I'm guessing your aversion might be pointing to your inner divine quality of dignity.[26] Do you feel averse to going into your weeping because that wouldn't fulfill your beautiful inner quality of dignity?

Tom: What came up was, *I should be better. I should know better.*

Mary Magdalene: Ah. A feeling of failure? Or not being good enough?

Tom: Yeah, that's pretty close.

Mary Magdalene: Not as good as you should be.

Tom: Yes.

Mary Magdalene: I'm guessing you're needing a sense of competence.

Tom: Yes.

Mary Magdalene: So, when you think about going into the sadness or the weepy quality, do you feel averse to doing that because you want a sense of competence, as a being and maybe as a man?

Tom: Yeah, "competence" is a good word.

Mary Magdalene: Yes.

Tom: I often don't feel competent.

Mary Magdalene: Yes. Your feeling of aversion is pointing to a longing in you. You're longing for connection with God, in this case through the quality of competence. Competence is truly realized in God. In your connection with God, you are competent. Do you have a sense of what I'm talking about?

Tom: I think so. If I knew I had competence in God, I'd be trusting.

Mary Magdalene: Yes. Let's do a practice of connecting with your own Godhood. It's not a psychological technique or even an imaginary process. It's very real.

Many people are programmed to believe they're not God. They believe God is somewhere else, up in the sky or wherever he lives, and that God is a "he." [Mary and Tom laugh.] They think, *God isn't here. And God isn't me, that's for sure.* That's what I would say is imaginary. I say God is everywhere, including being alive as you. God is also the mysterious, unknown, undefinable being that we contact as infinite, eternal Spirit. God is that too, but God is also everything else.

Do your best to connect with your own Godhood. Go inside and find the place in you that knows the competence you're longing for. When you find that place, let yourself merge with it. It might help to think of it as a pool of competence that you're diving into. Fill yourself up with the God-quality of competence, of being enough.

[Silence while Tom does what Mary asked.]

Tom: I have difficulty merging with it.

Mary Magdalene: What do you experience instead?

Tom: My head keeps popping in. There's a distance between the competence and my head.

Mary Magdalene: I'm guessing your head is trying to protect you, saying, *Don't do that! You're going to lose control. We won't be safe. Let me protect you. Just stay with me, and we'll figure this out.* Is that accurate?

Tom: Most likely, yes.

Mary Magdalene: My guess is you're needing safety. Safety to do this other thing that's unfamiliar and seems somehow threatening. Is that right?

Tom: Yes, yes.

Mary Magdalene: I want to speak to your head right now. Head, would you agree to stay present with us as we do this process and allow Tom to do the process while you observe? Then afterwards we'll check in with you and see what you thought about the process. Would that work for you?

Tom: OK.

Mary Magdalene: Great. Let's try again. Tom, somewhere inside you know what it is to have God's competence. This doesn't mean you are other than yourself. It just means you can locate your God-given competence, that "enoughness" that's yours. I invite you to find this place and merge with it, perhaps like diving into a pool of competence. Fill yourself with that competence, and notice what you experience.

[Silence while Tom follows Mary's instructions.]

Tom: I'm getting closer, but I still feel fear.

Mary Magdalene: What are you afraid of?

Tom: I might get lost.

Mary Magdalene: You said you often have this longing for competence. Is that right?

Tom: Yes.

Mary Magdalene: I suggest that you can't miss something unless you already know what it is to have it. Otherwise, how would you miss it?

Tom: That's right.

Mary Magdalene: Some part of you knows what it is to be competent. That's how you know it's missing. All I'm asking is to find that part of you that knows this competence.

Tom: I have a strange feeling my lack of competence is something I hide behind.

Mary Magdalene: Hmm. You're safe when you're hiding behind being incompetent. Then going into competence might feel vulnerable or unsafe.

Tom: Maybe that's it.

Mary Magdalene: To explore something new and unfamiliar may take courage. The old identity of *I'm not competent* might feel comfortable, like an old shoe.

Tom: Yes, yes.

Mary Magdalene: Are you willing to explore something new?

Tom: Yes.

Mary Magdalene: Then let's try. Let yourself go into that place that knows the quality of competence, being enough. Merge with that, and notice your experience.
　　[Silence as Tom does so.]

Tom: I'm trying hard to get in there, but it's such unknown territory for me.

Mary Magdalene: I'm guessing the pattern, "I'm not competent," which we're trying to unwind, goes very deep.

Tom: Yes, yes, it's been hanging around a long time.

Mary Magdalene: What are you trying to fulfill by not being competent?

Tom: I suppose then no one can say I failed.

Mary Magdalene: Yes. There's a kind of safety from being discovered as incompetent?

Tom: That's right.

Mary Magdalene: Yes. You think, *If I stay in the "I'm incompetent" zone and don't put myself out there, no one will really know that I may actually be incompetent.*

Tom: Right.

Mary Magdalene: So, it gives you emotional safety. Would you agree with that?

Tom: Yes. But no one will know that I'm competent either.

Mary Magdalene: You're not being seen for who you really are and how you express God in your own unique way. Is that right?

Tom: That's right.

Mary Magdalene: I also imagine that stepping back from being who you actually are interferes with your relationship with God.

Tom: Yes.

Mary Magdalene: So you must look at why. And the feelings are your guides. Somewhere along the line, probably in childhood, I imagine you started to doubt your competence. *Am I really competent? Am I really good enough? Am I as good as everyone else? Am I good enough to be loved, to be included?* You became afraid that others would question your competence and perhaps not love and include you. So, you assumed a mask to avoid showing yourself. Is that accurate?

Tom: That's pretty accurate. As you were speaking, this came up inside: *If I really let go into this, I might lose my mind*—if that makes any sense.

Mary Magdalene: Of course. When you let go of that part of your Beingness—the part connected to your competence—you withdrew into your mind. Now you live in your mind rather than in the fullness of who you are.

Tom: That's really true.

Mary Magdalene: You won't lose your mind if you open to your competence. Your mind will be rejoined with all of who you are. Your mind is a wonderful thing, but you don't have to live in it as an island of reclusiveness. How does that feel to you?

Tom: I want to go down into the competence.

Mary Magdalene: It may be competence all around—up, down, front, back, side, who knows? [laughs] Through and through. Ready to give it a try?

Tom: Yes, yes.

Mary Magdalene: I suggest you invite competence to come and show itself to you.
   [Silence as Tom tries the process again.]

Tom: There's a tingling in my body.

Mary Magdalene: Anything else?

Tom: I'm not so separated from it. Last time, my head was one place and competence was down there. Now it's almost part of me.

Mary Magdalene: It is part of you. Otherwise, you couldn't miss it.
   [More silence.]

Tom: I'm longing to experience something, but I'm not. [Tom begins to weep.]

Mary Magdalene: It sounds like you're experiencing sadness. That's something.

Tom: Yes, but it's not competence.

Mary Magdalene: Perhaps sadness comes first. Would you like to experience competence?

Tom: Yes.

Mary Magdalene: Then intend to do it. Ask with all your heart to be shown the experience of competence.

Tom: My head is getting in the way. *See? I told you you're not going to get through this.*

Mary Magdalene: Probably a very old voice, isn't it?

Tom: Yes. I'd like to set it aside, so I can continue inviting competence.

Mary Magdalene: Be strong with your mind: *Mind, I want you to relax. You will have a choice whether to believe this or not. But right now, I choose to experience this. Then I will come back to you.*

Tom: Yes. This resistance has been here a long time.

Mary Magdalene: How are you right now?

Tom: I want to invite competence in, to be one with it, merge with it.

Mary Magdalene: I think you're ready to turn this around now. Rather than inviting it in, I suggest you step into it. It's there waiting for you.

[Silence as Tom engages the process.]

Tom: I expected relief when I entered it, but I don't feel that.

Mary Magdalene: You may not. Let go of your expectations. Just be present for what is.

Tom: I guess I want to control it.

Mary Magdalene: Yes. Just notice. Be the observer. Merge with the place in you that knows competence and observe what happens.

[More silence as Tom engages the process.]

Mary Magdalene: What do you notice?

Tom: It's like walking into a pink atmosphere of warmth. I'm merging into it.

Mary Magdalene: Mm-hmm. How does it feel?

Tom: Like goodness. Like being surrounded.

Mary Magdalene: Does it bring up a feeling of peace?

Tom: Yes.

Mary Magdalene: Mm-hmm.

Tom: But there's a little anxiety in there. *You're not in there yet totally. Maybe you won't get in there totally.*

Mary Magdalene: Mm-hmm. Maybe you will or already are there.

Tom: [laughs, then sighs] Yeah. This whole thing has been around a long time.

Mary Magdalene: That's OK. We're very old beings. Would you like to merge with God in this particular way?

Tom: I would like to merge with God in a fuller way than I'm feeling right now.

Mary Magdalene: Do you think God is competent?

Tom: God is very competent.

Mary Magdalene: [chuckles] Would you like to experience that competence?

Tom: Yes.

Mary Magdalene: It's not about perfection—or that you can do anything you want. You're not going to go to the window and fly after this.

Tom: Shucks. [Mary and Tom laugh.]

Mary Magdalene: At least not without some flying lessons [laughs]. Because that wouldn't be very competent, would it?

Tom: No, it wouldn't. [Mary laughs heartily.]

Mary Magdalene: It means *you are enough.* You're filled with the same competence God fills everything with. You're not divorced from competence, separated, or cut off. That aspect of God is who you are, however it manifests through you. Would you like that?

Tom: Very much.

Mary Magdalene: Are you willing to open to it?

Tom: I'm willing to open to God's competence.

Mary Magdalene: I invite you to hold space for that right now. Perhaps it will feel like opening your heart. In the Indian tradition, there's a beautiful image of the monkey god Hanuman holding his chest open to reveal his heart. Perhaps that's what it might feel like to open your heart to God's competence. Let yourself do that now, however you experience that merging.

[Silence again as Tom engages the process]

Tom: I'm really trying. Maybe I'm trying too hard.

Mary Magdalene: Maybe. What do you feel?

Tom: The separateness of not being there.

Mary Magdalene: That is your identity. You identify as someone who's not competent, who wants to be competent but isn't there. Yes?

Tom: Yes.

Mary Magdalene: This work takes courage, which you have. I'm calling upon the courage in you to set that identity of non-competence aside for now. You're free to resume it in a minute if you choose. But for right now, set that aside. Know in this moment that you don't need that crutch, that mask. It's blocking you from what your heart desires. Take the mask off, set the crutch aside, and let go of your identity as someone who's not competent. Choose to walk into God's competence, to open yourself to God's competence.

[More silence as Tom engages the process]

Loving the Resistance

Tom: It's not happening.

Mary Magdalene: Then there's more that's blocking it. This will be your area of exploration, to feel and go into the resistance, so you can heal it. The resistance is like a hurting child, which you can't just walk away from or overcome by clobbering it [laughs]. Yet most humans try to do that.

You must become a lover here—a lover of your resistance. You must open up to those hurting child parts of yourself that are afraid to let go because they've had painful experiences. You must reassure, love, embrace, and carry them with you into this place of competence. But first befriend them. You do that through feeling. Does that make sense to you?

Tom: Yes.

Mary Magdalene: It takes courage to notice your feelings and fears. The blockage is usually fear. Don't try to make the fear go away. Embrace it instead.

Tom: I want to make the fear go away, to move it aside.

Mary Magdalene: Yes, so you can be competent, right? [Mary and Tom laugh.] This isn't about you being competent. This is about opening to God's competence, which relieves you of having to be competent or incompetent. You're experiencing the ocean of God's competence and bringing that into your moment-to-moment choices.

There's a timing to this. Perhaps this is not the time for you
to open. Perhaps you don't have the safety in this moment because you're being observed, and this is being recorded (and will be
shared with others). That's fine. Your inherent being is protecting
you. It may happen at another time, in a different setting, perhaps
later today or in a few days when you feel comfortable and safe.
We've planted seeds.

Tom: Yes. When I'm alone, do I just go through the same process?
I really want to experience God's competence.

Mary Magdalene: Yes. Begin by inviting yourself to fully experience your resistance. If your resistance is old beliefs, love the
beliefs. If it's feelings, love the feelings. That's how you heal the
splintered-off parts of yourself that are in pain.

The Prison of Mind

Mary Magdalene: This process may seem like a great deal of work
at first if you're not used to it. But the benefits are immense: freedom, liberation, joy. I assure you, the effort is so worth it.

Tom: I long for that.

Mary Magdalene: Yes. You're breaking out of the prison of your
mind, which you've erected yourself, a prison that causes tremendous suffering. The route back is through your feelings and the
beautiful divinity within you that those feelings are trying to reconnect you with.

Somewhere inside, a young boy still lives. That boy existed before he was ever told he was incompetent. He didn't question his competence. He practiced for months and months to learn how to walk with no doubt that he would accomplish it. You accomplished so many things. That boy can't wait to be found again. That boy will open you to chambers of yourself where you'll celebrate and dance.

Tom: Mmm . . .

Mary Magdalene: That boy wants to rejoin your adult self right now. And you won't regress to being nine months old. [Mary and Tom laugh.] Unless you choose to do so, which you may on certain occasions. [Mary laughs again.]

When you connect with this part of yourself, the divinity within, your reality will change. The suffering in your mind will change. The feeling of carrying the weight of the world will change. Your longing to experience God's competence (and your apparent incapacity to do so), all of that will change. Your practical life will also change.

You didn't come here to have a perfect practical life. You came here to know God in the midst of all the practicalities of life, and you're doing that.

Tom: I want to experience all of this. At the same time, I regret that I haven't been able to in our session.

Mary Magdalene: Let yourself regret. That regret is a wonderful thing because it will grow and heal you. Sadly, many of you have learned that you shouldn't feel regret. You think you're not being competent if you regret [laughs]. This is so unfortunate and inaccurate. Regret is one of the healthiest things there is. When you allow it, you don't stay stuck in the regret. If you experience the regret to its depths, it moves on, and you're stronger because of it.

By allowing regret, you allow the Feminine, which guides you back to the Masculine. It will guide you to competence, and your competence will grow. This is the beautiful dance of the Feminine and the Masculine. The Feminine loves the Masculine and loves to support the Masculine. Open to the riches of the Feminine. You will not regret it, I assure you.

I sense we've covered a great deal, and there is fullness at this point. But I want to check in with you once again. How are you doing?

Tom: [weeping] I'm sad that I didn't accomplish what I wanted to do.

Mary Magdalene: Look what you've accomplished. You're feeling your sadness and allowing your tears, which you weren't able to do at the beginning of this session. Your sadness is guiding and helping you. Embrace her. Open to the sadness. She will guide you.

Tom: I feel like I've let you and Yeshua down. You want me to go through this, and I haven't.

Mary Magdalene: Would you like to hear from us about that?

Tom: Yes.

Mary Magdalene: [laughs] I'm not let down at all. I absolutely trust this process. It's not necessarily a snap of your fingers, a quick fix, "Wham, bam, thank you, ma'am." [Mary and Tom laugh.]

I have immense gratitude to you for your openness to work at this tremendously deep level. Many will feel a great resonance and appreciation for your process as you go through it so meticulously, step by step because they need all those steps too. I have no doubt that you'll open to this at the perfect time. I see the beauty of you expressing your sadness at the end and opening to the Feminine through that. You may not see it yet, but it's very clear to me.

Tom: Thank you.

Mary Magdalene: Humanity has been closed to the Feminine for what seems like eons. This huge burden is a real structure in consciousness that cannot be thrown overboard in a split second [laughs]. That's possible, but most likely the process will happen step by step to provide the God-safety that humans need in order to change. From my perspective (and I know I speak for Yeshua too) you're changing at tremendous speed. If you could see that, you would be in awe and full of respect, as are we.

Tom: Thank you. Thank you very much.

Mary Magdalene: We love you so much, and we're not giving up. [Mary and Tom laugh.] Don't get too serious about it, please [laughs].

Tom: I'm glad you're not giving up.

Mary Magdalene: How could we? We love you so much. Thank you for this wonderful time we've had together.

Tom: Thank you, thank you. And thank Yeshua too.

Mary Magdalene: Absolutely. In great love, we leave you now.

Tom: We'll see you.

Mary Magdalene: Indeed.

THIRTEEN

The Courage to Be with Fear

[Eighteen months later]

Yeshua: Hello, beloved. This is Yeshua. It's been quite a while.

Tom: Hello, Yeshua. It sure has been a long time.

Yeshua: I'm glad we're resuming.

Tom: So am I.

Yeshua: I thank you for this service, which you're doing on behalf of many. Thank you for staying with me, with us, in this practice, and for your trust in us to help and guide you.

Tom: I thank you, Yeshua and Mary Magdalene, for hanging in with me. I'm a slow learner, I guess. After our last conversation, I was sad that I didn't get through everything. Our session was very deep, spiraling. Every time Mary asked me to imagine something, a fear arose—many layers of fear. Thank you for sticking with me.

Yeshua: You are most welcome. It's our great joy and honor to do so. May I say something about your fear?

Tom: Yes.

Yeshua: The third-dimensional reality is largely predicated on fear. Some in your spiritual world put forth the idea that if you're spiritual, you won't experience fear. Or perhaps you'll go beyond fear. That's unlikely as long as you're in the third dimension because fear is a profound part of this dimension.

Those who believe that spirituality eliminates fear often end up cutting off and suppressing their fear, either intentionally or unknowingly. Some are afraid to acknowledge they have fear—to themselves or to others. Out of fear! [laughs] They think fear means they're not spiritual, but that's not the case at all. Fear means you're experiencing third-dimensional reality.

It takes courage to experience third-dimensional reality. This is not an easy place. It's a place of great suffering, pain, and death. It also takes love. If you don't experience fear, you aren't in touch with love. Love opens the heart. Cutting off fear closes down the heart.

As I've said before, you came here to experience God manifesting as third-dimensional reality, which requires opening yourself to third-dimensional reality, including fear. Mary Magdalene was guiding you through that process of opening, and that's what you were doing.

I suspect you think you shouldn't have been feeling fear and that others in this process might not feel fear. You're judging yourself as being lesser than, unworthy, or not good enough because you were feeling fear [chuckles]. That's like saying you're not good enough because you experience life, Earth, or the third dimension itself.

This bears repeating. This is exactly what you came to experience: the third dimension as a manifestation of God. Not as something separate from God or something that fell, with God remaining "up there" while you're "down here." [Tom laughs.] All this *is*

God. God is everything, and this is God, which means you are God. You're not separate.

This orientation I'm pointing to isn't something simply to be believed the way a child believes in Santa Claus. If you take it that way, you will be led to the same place that belief has always led you [laughs]. Rather than a belief in your mind, this must be your actual lived experience, which happens through embracing your reality fully, including fear.

Most people in your world have been taught the opposite, that they shouldn't have fear. If they do, they should not let others know. *Try to act like you don't have fear. Even convince yourself you don't have it.* That's a false belief that takes you away from what you came here to do.

If you're experiencing the third dimension, you're going to experience fear, but it doesn't have to separate you from God. In fact, rightly understood, fear will guide you back to union with God. Fear shows you the places deep within you where you've separated from God. It can lead you to reconnecting with God from the core of your being.

Acknowledging and opening to fear can be one of your greatest allies, if you have the tools to make use of it. But you've been trained to be afraid of fear [laughs]. To go beyond the fear of fear takes trust and courage. Mary Magdalene was showing you that path, and you were opening yourself to it. But a learning process is involved because you've been trained so differently, and that training has been powerful.

Let's imagine you're a parent of a young boy, perhaps six years old and in elementary school. A highly-trained mathematician explains to your son, "At some point you're going to learn calculus, and it will be a wonderful gift and tool."

"I don't know what you're talking about," your son replies [laughs]. Would you judge your son for not knowing what calculus is or how to do it?

Tom: No, I wouldn't judge him at all.

Yeshua: Would you think there's something the matter with him or that maybe he isn't good enough?

Tom: If it were me, I would have thought that. [Yeshua and Tom laugh.]

Yeshua: Yes. But if this was your son, what would you think?

Tom: I wouldn't be surprised that he wouldn't know calculus.

Yeshua: Exactly. That would be natural to who he is and his stage of development.

Tom: Very much so, yes.

Yeshua: This is what you must also do with yourself.

Tom: As you're speaking now about fear, I've felt a release in my shoulders.

Yeshua: That's an excellent sign—and an excellent sign that you noticed it.

Tom: In other conversations you often asked me, "How is it for you now? How do you feel?", and I'd quickly jump to another topic. I realize I was avoiding the question.

I had a dream recently where a friend asked me, "Tom, how are you?"

"I gave a retreat a couple of weeks ago," I replied.

We moved to another room, and he asked me again, "How are you?"

"I gave a retreat," I said. I never listened. That's so often what I've done. I haven't responded to your questions about how I am inside. My head takes me to something else—to an agenda I think I should be on [laughs].

Yeshua: Do you know why you do that?

Tom: Probably out of fear.

Yeshua: Exactly. What do you fear?

Tom: Exposing myself or something like that.

You Were Taught Guilt

Tom: I had an experience yesterday related to fear and not being enough. I was looking out the window. The sun was shining, we had brand-new snow, and the creek was running. I looked at the tree and thought, *You're a tree, and you're enough, just as you are, being a tree.* Then I looked at the creek. *You're enough, just as you are.* Then the snow. *You're enough, just as you are.* Then I said to myself, *Why can't I be enough just the way I am? What's stopping me from being OK just the way I am?*

Later that night in meditation, I chose to be with my fear, following Mary Magdalene's instruction. As I explored my bodily sensations, I felt an uncomfortable tingling all over my body. I stayed with it, and a feeling of guilt washed over me. *There are so many things I've said and done that I'm not proud of. How can I be enough? How can God be within me if I've done all these things?*

I sat with the guilt, just being with it. And again, fear. After I finished, I told Ann about my experience of fear and guilt. "If I'm going to be honest with Yeshua and Mary Magdalene, I need to tell all of this to them." I expected to be agitated overnight because of this, but I wasn't. I was at peace. [Yeshua chuckles.]

This morning, I felt new, like it's a new beginning. I really want to be honest with myself and with you as we begin again.

Yeshua: You've done powerful work with powerful results. You are beautifully on track, and yes, it begins with being real. You've been trained that you shouldn't feel your body, energy, sexuality, or feelings, as if it's wrong or even dangerous to do so. A young baby, a newborn, doesn't come into this realm afraid of its body, feelings, energy, or sex. There *are* fears that are instinctual, such as the fear of death or danger. But the fears you're describing aren't instinctual; they're instilled and trained, as is the fear that something is the matter with you, you're not good enough, you've sinned, you've made unforgivable mistakes, or you're damned. Are you following?

Tom: Yes.

Yeshua: You didn't come into this life with any of that, unless you're carrying past-life memories (which is possible), or there's a soul continuation of certain beliefs.

Tom: I was wondering if these fears came from a past life.

Yeshua: It's possible. But do you understand the difference between what is natural and what is learned?

Tom: Yes.

Yeshua: You're suffering from things you've learned, that have been instilled, and you've accepted them as truth. Now you struggle greatly. Guilt arises if you experience your body, feelings, energy, or sexuality. If you've made mistakes or have regrets, you think you've done something wrong, bad, or irredeemable, and you must hide. It's not safe to show yourself—or others or God—what you've done because you'll be punished. Perhaps you'll lose love or respect or be excluded. Or you may suffer after this life by not going to heaven or by going to hell. Catholicism probably reinforced such ideas of badness, wrongness, guilt, and sin—accompanied by the need to hide. So, you're struggling with all of this. Does this feel accurate to you?

Tom: Yes, very accurate.

The Hero's Journey

Yeshua: Fundamentally, this social training is predicated on a denial of the Feminine. It's saying your body, energy, sexuality, and emotions should be kept under lock and key or certainly controlled at all costs. The Masculine must dominate in you. You must live in your mind, supported by your will and power center.

Can you feel that?

Tom: That's what I've been doing, yes.

Yeshua: It's what humanity has been doing. Men and women both receive this indoctrination, though it manifests for each in somewhat different ways. The root is the same, and the damage is immense.

Humanity came to Earth and the third dimension to experience and *love* the Feminine, to experience the union of the Masculine and the Feminine as manifestations of God. Sadly, humanity has gotten quite off track with that.

Presently, humanity is at a great turning point of shifting this dynamic and opening to the Feminine, men and women alike. This is huge. I would say the work is more difficult for men. The men involved in this work are heroes. You're one of them. I say that knowing you may not accept that, but it's my truth. I say it to plant the seed and support you in whatever way it can.

You began your hero's journey when you said, "I'm not in agreement with what's happening within the Catholic church, even though I'm a priest." You began walking your own path, following your own truth, and moving away from the denial of the Feminine. The obvious sign is that you knew you wanted to be with a beloved woman and to take her as your wife. That was your truth. Is this so?

Tom: Yes, yes. It brings tears to my eyes. Last night Ann and I gave each other a hug and kiss goodnight, and she said, "You are worthy. You are precious, more than a million times over. I left all the men I knew and all the men I'm going to know for you." This morning she quoted something to me she'd read: "I love you unconditionally. Your action is irrelevant."

Yeshua: You chose wisely.

Tom: We're working at this together.

Yeshua: Indeed, for your whole life. You're one of the leaders, which doesn't mean being a president of a country or something like that. It means you're a leader of the light, which happens in your heart, being, and soul. The masses may not recognize you. It's about what you're living inside yourself.

Tom: Thank you. I want to continue in that journey.

Before this session, I told Mercedes I needed more time to go over the transcripts of our previous sessions. Mercedes asked, "Are you afraid because you want to be perfect?" I wept when I heard that because it's true.

Yeshua: Precisely. You see, being fearful is not being weak, just human. [Yeshua and Tom laugh.] It's like saying you're weak if you're hungry. Hunger is just your body's way of letting you know you need nutrition. Fear is your being's way of letting you know you need a God-connection. Let's go into that God-connection. Are you open to doing that?

Tom: Yes, I am. I'm wondering, how can God be within me if I've done all these things that might be wrong?

Yeshua: It's not possible if you keep thinking that way [laughs]. Your judgment that wrongness even exists is creating a reality where, of course, God would reject you [more laughter].

Tom: I want to eliminate that and just be with the process here.

Yeshua: You've created a God who rejects people because they're wrong. That is not my God. That's the God of the Church.

Tom: Yes, yes.

Yeshua: That God was created by human beings for a specific purpose: to control. If human beings hate themselves or think they're sinners (bad and evil), then they need authorities to redeem them, and they give their power to those authorities. Yes?

Tom: Yes, yes.

Yeshua: This is not God. This is human control. We will set that God aside because that is not the God I speak of or know.

Tom: The God you know is the God I want to be with.

Yeshua: Yes. Let's do that.

Tom: OK.

You're a Beautiful Being with Power

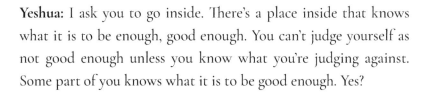

Yeshua: I ask you to go inside. There's a place inside that knows what it is to be enough, good enough. You can't judge yourself as not good enough unless you know what you're judging against. Some part of you knows what it is to be good enough. Yes?

Tom: Yes.

Yeshua: Give yourself permission to go to that part that knows what it is to be good enough: that place of good-enoughness inside. Let yourself go into it, like entering a chamber. Fill up with good-enoughness, and notice what you experience.

    [Silence as Tom responds]

Tom: In my throat and solar plexus, I feel I want to weep.

Yeshua: I recommend letting yourself weep if you feel moved to do so.
  [Silence again]

Tom: I've gone deeper into that weepy feeling. There's a shield around me. I don't know if it's protecting me or stopping me from going in.

Yeshua: Is there fear there?

Tom: Most probably that's what it is.

Yeshua: What are you afraid may happen if you let yourself go into the good-enoughness?
  [Silence as Tom checks inside]

Tom: I'm not sure what I'm afraid of right now.

Yeshua: OK. Just be with that. Being unsure is fine.
  [Silence]
  Open to the good-enoughness.
  [Silence]

Tom: I'm trying to put words to my feelings: *I judge others like I judge myself.*

Yeshua: Of course. Are you judging yourself right now?

Tom: I think I am.

Yeshua: Say the judgments out loud.

Tom: I'm not good enough. I can't do this.

Yeshua: There's fear, and you need confidence that you can do this. Is that true?

Tom: It would help to have confidence [laughs].

Yeshua: That's not a clear response. It either is so or it is not. It's fine if it's not.

Tom: It's probably confidence that I'm able to do this.

Yeshua: Self-confidence.

Tom: Yes. Faith in myself that I can do this.

Yeshua: Let's go there—to the part of you that knows what it is to have self-confidence and faith in yourself. Can you find that place?

Tom: It's been rare in my life, Yeshua.

Yeshua: I'm not looking for experience. This is a pure quality, which doesn't depend on any experience whatsoever; it's beyond experience. In you lives the pure essence of self-confidence and faith in yourself. Can you find that?
   [Silence]

Tom: I have a burning feeling in my chest.

Yeshua: Is it painful or pleasurable?

Tom: Again, there's a feeling of needing to weep.

Yeshua: Perhaps that's a sign when you deeply connect with yourself and God. What do you think?

Tom: Yes, I think it is.

Yeshua: I'm guessing that in the past you've taken that weepy feeling as a kind of wrongness or weakness on your part. Is that so?

Tom: Yes.

Yeshua: Do you see what an inner battle you're struggling with?

Tom: There's tingling around my body again and warmth inside. It's like an egg [laughs].

Yeshua: Yes. It sounds like you're connecting with your energy field. I take that as a wonderful sign of coming to life. Your ideas have been deadening you. You're overcoming them by empowering your inner Feminine. You've been convinced that you're a weak person, which is not the case at all, but it will continue to be so as long as you believe it. Does that make sense to you?

Tom: Yes, yes.

Yeshua: It sounds like you're finding your strength, which may be unfamiliar. Is that so?

Tom: That's right.

Yeshua: The programming has been effective at removing your power. But now you're reclaiming your power. This is what power feels like.

Tom: I want to live in that power.

Yeshua: I invite you to do so and welcome you there. Welcome to your power. You're a beautiful being with power.

We've done very deep work, and I sense this may be a good place to rest for now.

Tom: Yes, I'm going to remember this feeling and experience. I want to bask in it and stay in it.

Yeshua: Perfect.

Tom: Thank you so much, Yeshua.

Yeshua: It's my great pleasure. I love you profoundly.

Tom: And I love you. Say hello to Mary Magdalene.

Yeshua: Say hello to Ann.

Tom: I'll do that. Thank you.

Yeshua: Blessings, my dear one.

Tom: Blessings.

FOURTEEN

Coming Home

Yeshua: Hello, dear one. This is Yeshua returning again. I'm so glad to continue our process and dialogue.

Tom: I'm glad you're back, Yeshua. Thank you for your love and patience with me.

Yeshua: It is my joy and honor.

Tom: Thank you especially for responding to my issues of fear and guilt and for guiding me to God, my enoughness, and self-confidence.

Yeshua: It is a great joy. You're doing the soul work you came to do. To join someone in that process is a wonderful thing.

Tom: Thank you. I feel weepy just hearing you say that.
    Since our last meeting, I've been reflecting on our process. I'd like to relate what I've gone through.

Yeshua: Yes.

Tom: A couple of days ago, I listened to one of my favorite songs, "Bring Him Home," from Les Misérables, which touches me deeply. After the song ended, Ann asked, "Why do you like that song so much?" Teary and emotional, I responded, "Because I want to come home. I want to connect with God." [Tom starts weeping.]

Yeshua: Yes.

Tom: To connect with my "I am enoughness." I've been wanting that all along.

Yeshua: Yes.

Tom: Bring me home inside myself where God resides. Bring me home to God in manifestation, in the trees and the flowers, the sky, the house next door, and people—even people I have trouble with.

Yeshua: Yes.

Tom: I've been reflecting on what my obstacles are to getting in touch with God within me. Perhaps I'm still thinking of a God elsewhere, the old programming of a physical God somewhere up in the sky.

Yeshua: Exactly!

Tom: Yet, I've been telling everyone, "God isn't up in the sky. God is everywhere and in you and me." But I never really knew what that meant for me. I recalled you saying, "Perhaps weeping is one of your signs when you connect with God."

Yeshua: Yes.

Tom: I think that's true. I've experienced that numerous times.

Yeshua: Of course.

Tom: Suddenly, I had a kind of aha: *The answer to connecting with God is in the feelings, the felt sense, even the tears.*

Yeshua: Yes!

Tom: A little later I shared my experience with Ann. I was in tears. I was about to explain my tears (which was my head taking over), and she said, "Don't move on. Stay with the feeling."

Yeshua: [laughs] Wise counsel.

Tom: And I did.

Yeshua: This is so wonderful.

Tom: Later on I remembered again how Mercedes asked if I was feeling afraid to return to the channeling because I thought I'd failed. Again, I began to weep. I'd connected with a feeling, which touched my heart.

Yeshua: That's a great example. You felt fear around not being enough, not being good enough or perfect enough. The fear was running you, and you were running from it. But when you turned and opened to the fear, it took you to your God-connection.

Tom: Yes, yes, yes.

Yeshua: In that God-connection, there's no question that you're enough, that you're perfect, manifesting just as you are.

Tom: Yes, yes.

Yeshua: This is a great demonstration! This is exactly what we've been hoping to draw you into further. I'm delighted to hear your report and description.

Tom: Thank you.

All of You Is God

Tom: Like you said, this is my soul path; it's what I came here for.

Yeshua: Absolutely. It's true for all beings in the third dimension.

In the third dimension, you think you're separate from God, that you exist and God exists, as if they are two different things. That yearning to go home is a yearning to reconnect with God. All souls share this yearning for God, though they may not be conscious of it. Yearning generally takes the form of seeking—seeking wealth, love, success, security. Ultimately, what's underneath is a seeking for God.

You've been in touch with your seeking for God at a deeper level than the majority of beings. This yearning originally drew you to become a priest and also drew you beyond the priesthood onto the path you've walked since.

Tom: Mary Magdalene said that everything we do is to get in touch with a part of our divinity, the beauty within us. She asked, "What part of your divinity were you looking for when you identified with not being competent, not being enough?" It was emotional safety, not being seen as a failure. But in making the choice to hide my competence, I also gave up being seen as who I really am and my unique way of expressing God.

Yeshua: The truth is you can't help but be who you are and express God in your unique way. But like all third-dimensional beings, you have made a profoundly deep assumption that you're separate from God. That assumption is what separates you from all the ways God is manifesting as you.

I want to plant this seed: God is not within you. You are within God [laughs]. All of you is God. Nothing is exempt.

To go within is a useful process when people have assumed a position of separation from God (which is generally the case in the third dimension). Going within supports the process of reconnecting with God. But God isn't within you any more than God is up in the sky, sitting on a throne. These are both concepts and visions of separateness. Everything is in God.

God chose to manifest God's Beingness as *all that is*, including all of you [laughs]. Not just flowers and snowflakes but all of you and all beings. Going within can be useful, however, for connecting with the "all-ness" of God.

Beyond Duality

Tom: Your words bring up a wonderful feeling, but a little bit of "if" popped up. If somebody is doing something vicious, I'd assume something was wrong, but God doesn't see things like that.

Yeshua: No. Right and wrong is a third-dimensional construct.

Tom: Can you explain that further?

Yeshua: In the third dimension, beings are given free will. They need the full range of possibilities to experience free will and learn the ramifications of different choices. This grand design of creation produces manifestation in its current form.

Another thread in the fabric of third-dimensional consciousness is duality. Things are seen through the lens of two extremes or poles. There's goodness-badness, rightness-wrongness, appropriate-inappropriate, should-shouldn't, and many other variations. They all express the same fundamental concept.

In the midst of this, you think your job is to discern between these poles. Some people believe their job is to do the right thing; others think it's to do the wrong thing. But really, your job is to go beyond the system of duality altogether.

When you go beyond your mental fascination with rightness or wrongness, you fall into the heart, where there is neither rightness nor wrongness but simply experience, lessons, and growth.

Eventually, you come to understand that the program of judging right or wrong is a block that keeps you from the heart and from the growth that's possible from experience. Ultimately, this programming keeps you from harvesting the wisdom of the third dimension, which is to learn about power.

The third dimension is a great school for learning about power. Most of the third dimension is based on "me versus you": those who have power versus those who don't. Again, a dualistic model. Seeing things as right or wrong serves those who have power; it's a way to get others to give their power away. True power resides in the marriage of the heart and the higher mind. Focusing on right and wrong keeps people out of their heart and higher mind—and thus disempowered.

Eventually, people can't help but connect with their soul and their soul path, which will move them to question the whole program of right or wrong and of living exclusively in the mind. The program of right/wrong and living in the mind leaves people hungry for the spiritual connection of the heart. This hunger starts to shift people into their heart regardless of the programming instilled by those in power.

Once empowered through this shift into the heart, people will start to see the shallowness and hollowness of right/wrong thinking and living in the mind. They will recognize the motivation behind it: to maintain power with the few and to convince the many to give away their power.

You cannot stop Spirit. You cannot stop the soul. You might waylay it for a time or detour it though. Humanity has been on a great detour. But you could also say the detour has been perfect, in its own way, as a great process of learning about power.

As humanity tires of this old program and starts to disregard its messages, one by one, people will awaken to the heart, as you're describing. That will lead people to a different kind of power. This is a sign of opening to the next dimension, the fourth dimension.

In the fourth dimension, power isn't held as "me versus you." It's held as *me with you, me and you*. My power is only powerful to the extent it includes the all; it includes me, and it includes all beings. We don't need to be in competition. We don't need to be claiming power over others. Rather, we can be in power with others.

At that point right and wrong will become a humorous matter, an earlier stage of consciousness, much as adults see a child's relationship to Santa Claus—it served a purpose at an earlier stage but no longer at the current stage. Does that answer your question?

Tom: Yes, it does.

The Consciousness of the Heart

Yeshua: Mary Magdalene has clarified a path to guide people out of right/wrong thinking and into the consciousness of the heart. The teaching is simple yet profound and deeply supportive of humanity's growth. Humanity needs this to open to the next stage. Mary is a master of the heart and a great lover of humanity.

Tom: Just by speaking to her I can sense that.

Yeshua: It's her soul path to help in that way.

Tom: When I first heard Mercedes channeling Mary Magdalene and you, I knew I wanted to talk with the two of you.

Yeshua: This is your great strength. You don't see it in yourself, but it's so obvious to us. You're a great leader because you *see* and have the courage to open yourself to what you see. You *know* at a deep level and have the courage to follow that knowledge. We honor your strength.

Tom: Thank you. It humbles me to hear that.

Yeshua: Going through this process with us in these sessions, in a way that will serve so many, is part of your leadership. We're so grateful for what you've provided and made possible.

Uniting Masculine and Feminine

Tom: In the Bible, it says, "If you love me keep my commandments. And I will ask the Father, and he will give you another advocate to help you and be with you forever—the Spirit of Truth."[27] Did you actually say that? If you did, what did you mean?

Yeshua: This saying occurred in a very different time. I spoke to help the people, at that time in ways that made sense to them. The idea of consciousness (which is the principle of the Masculine and of Father God) was a new idea then. People were much more connected to the Mother aspect of God. They needed help opening to the idea of consciousness and light. My soul path in that incarnation and ever since was to support that opening.

Much of humanity still struggles to connect with the transcendent aspect of God, the pure light of truth, the absolute aspect of God. But things are different now. Much has been done, at least at a foundational level, to make that available to those who are ready.

The next phase is to bring in the union of the Masculine and the Feminine because the Feminine has suffered at the hands of the Masculine. This is true spiritually as well as practically. Now there is a new opening in the spiritual development and evolution of humanity.

What spoke to people at the time the Bible was written can be easily misinterpreted because humanity isn't at that same moment. The thinking, consciousness, awareness, and needs aren't the same—though the fundamental truth behind the words remains. Does that answer your question?

Tom: Yes, it does. Spirit is nudging me through my feelings and intuition as I receive answers from my own being.

Yeshua: I support that. Don't overthink these things. If they serve you, let them serve you. If they don't, let them flow by.

Tom: As you say, the important thing is not to give authority to somebody else for my truth.

Yeshua: Yes. From the time you left the priesthood, you rose to make a difficult choice. You chose exactly what we're talking about, your own obvious truth despite great pressures to do otherwise.

Finding Your Own Enoughness

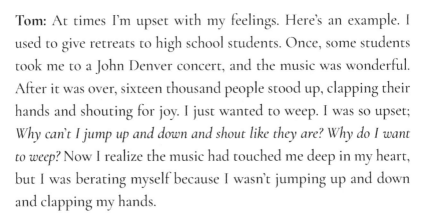

Tom: At times I'm upset with my feelings. Here's an example. I used to give retreats to high school students. Once, some students took me to a John Denver concert, and the music was wonderful. After it was over, sixteen thousand people stood up, clapping their hands and shouting for joy. I just wanted to weep. I was so upset; *Why can't I jump up and down and shout like they are? Why do I want to weep?* Now I realize the music had touched me deep in my heart, but I was berating myself because I wasn't jumping up and down and clapping my hands.

Yeshua: That was *their* way of expressing: *You've connected me to God, to my God-self, the God-being I long to connect with.* Weeping was your way. There's no need to compare yourself with anyone else. You were all expressing in your own perfect form.

Tom: Many times I expect myself to be something other than what I am.

Yeshua: Yes. That's part of the program of *not good-enoughness* [laughs]. *I shouldn't be me. I should be what someone else is manifesting.* But that's their enoughness. Each of you has your own version of enoughness.

Tom: Maybe I'm wanting to be honored or recognized as succeeding. Ann certainly recognizes that in me. I feel you've acknowledged me by asking me to do this and thanking me for doing so, along with your love and patience with me.
[pause]
Actually, that's all I have for today.

Yeshua: Yes. Eventually the need for speech falls away as we swim in the beautiful ocean of God-connection. I sense this has happened.

Tom: Yes. I spoke to Mercedes earlier. We agreed that we've been engaging in two processes: my initial questions, some of which I still haven't asked, and my going within on my own journey. She said, "Whatever is still there as a question, you can ask." But I want to attend to my own journey first.

Yeshua: I'm very happy to do both of these things with you. Both are important.
I'm sensing a resting place for now.

Tom: Yes. I feel honored to be here with you. I really do.

Yeshua: It's a joy to be with you.

Tom: Thank you.

Yeshua: Blessings, blessings, blessings.

Tom: Blessings to you and to Mary Magdalene. I heard a Mayan phrase, *In Lak'ech*, which means "I am another you."

Yeshua: Yes. And so it is.

Tom: Thank you.

Yeshua: We leave you for a time, to resume again at another time.

Tom: Yes. Thank you.

FIFTEEN

The Maze of Mind

Yeshua: Hello, beloved. This is Yeshua. I'm happy to be with you today. How are you?

Tom: Thank you so much, Yeshua, for being present and for your encouragement, love, and support. It's good to be back with you. I must admit, I'm very anxious about this conversation.

Yeshua: What is causing you anxiety?

Tom: This past while hasn't been easy. Just as I think I've made a major step on my journey, my mind says, *Not so fast. You're not really doing this.*

In our last conversation, you said I opened to my fear of not being good enough and that turning toward my fear took me into God-connection. You added, "In that God-connection, there's no question that you're enough, that you're completely perfect, manifesting just as you are."

Afterwards, I wondered, *Is it all true? Did I really do the process that Yeshua and Mary Magdalene wanted? Did I truly feel the OK-ness, the yes-ness that Yeshua was pointing to?* I'm also afraid that I've described the Church wrongly in some of our conversations. And I feel worried for the sake of others. *Am I asking the right questions?*

I've been experiencing an energy on the surface of my body. It happens suddenly throughout the day. But when I try to open to the feeling, I can't enter it. *Is this a feeling of closeness to God, or is it some fear?* I'm not sure.

During an evening meditation, pain came into the pit of my stomach. I tried to follow the process you've been guiding me in by asking, *What's the fear here?* A question came in response: *Do I have feelings of love for Ann?* That hit me hard. I tried to stay with the pain and the energy in my body as I thought about love.

So often I've said to God and Jesus, "I love you." But did I ever have feelings of love when I said it? With Ann, I really love her. Yet at that point, I wasn't having feelings of love in our relationship. The feeling was heavy. *Did I really love her?*

Then came an added fear: I was afraid to tell her. I tried to be with that fear, but I felt overwhelmed. I knew if I didn't tell her, I wouldn't be at peace inside.

Later I told Ann I loved her very much, but somehow I wasn't feeling that love, which concerned me. I told her I had no intention of leaving her. I affirmed how much she means to me. I also shared that I was questioning if I ever feel love for others, even God and Jesus, even though I really intend that love.

Ann was gentle and caring in her response. "Did you ever have feelings of love for me?" she asked.

"Yes, I did," I replied.

We embraced and she asked me, "Do you feel afraid of not being able to love at all?" That resonated with me. I know that love and fear can't be in the same place.

Yeshua: Tom, I must interrupt you. This is what happens when you live in your mind. It's a hell.

Tom: Yes.

Yeshua: You don't have to tell me all the ins and outs of how you live in your mind [laughs]. It's simply a hell realm. [Tom laughs.]

Tom: I told Ann, "I'm living too much in my head. My head has taken over my whole being."

Yeshua: Yes. Even your relationship to your feelings exists in your mind. Now you're trying to navigate your feelings from your mind. It can't be done, Tom.

Tom: Yes. Last night I asked my dream to give me some clarification.

Yeshua: Tom, you don't need information. You don't need understanding. You need to get into your heart. It's not going to happen through your mind in any way, shape, or form.

Tom: Perhaps my anxiety has to do with wanting to clear up a few things with you. I still have lingering questions about the Eucharist and Peter's role in the Church.

Yeshua: What would you like of me now, Tom?

Tom: There's still a little bit of angst within me, but earlier in the week it was like a panic.

Yeshua: What is true of you right now?

Tom: I guess what I want to say is this: if I'm so slow and have all these difficulties, how can you ask me to do all this for other people?

Yeshua: Tom, it's not your job to judge yourself.

Tom: Pardon me?

Yeshua: This is your role. You've been given this by Spirit.

Tom: [weeping] I'm honored, and I want to do this. But a trigger keeps coming up, asking, *Why me?*

Yeshua: Why not you?

Tom: Because there are millions of others who are better than I am. I know you told me we all manifest in our own way. And Ann says she loves me the way I am.

Yeshua: Those are your strategies to try to prop yourself up. But they don't help, do they?

Tom: I still have angst within my chest.

Yeshua: Yes, because you're not dealing with the root. You're just putting on your fix-it hat with these aphorisms. Kind of like what you teach in Sunday school to children, right? [laughs]

Tom: There's more. Last night in my dream . . .

Yeshua: No, Tom, we're not going there. I don't care about your dreams. I don't care about your thoughts. I care about what's alive in you now. Can we be with that?

You Are Both Perfect and Imperfect

Tom: I have to mention something else. As a priest I had an affair with a woman. I still have all kinds of guilt around it. Ann knows about it. I told her before we got married. Anyhow, that's one last thing that might be bugging me.

Yeshua: Do you think that has something to do with our work together?

Tom: I guess it's part of my not being perfect and another reason why I wonder how you could ask me to do this. Because I've done all kinds of stupid things.

Yeshua: [laughs] You would be of no value to me if you were perfect. I'd be having a conversation with God! [Yeshua and Tom laugh.] You're human, and that's perfect.

Tom: [laughs] Thank you.

Yeshua: Sadly, you have great judgment about yourself for being human. It appears you see that as a great failing. How beautiful that you loved a woman and followed your heart! There may be aspects of the way you went about it that you regret or wish you'd done differently. That's a very human sentiment. Regret grows the being.

No human comes to this realm to be perfect. If you were perfect you wouldn't be manifesting here in the third dimension. You're here, as are all third-dimensional beings, to grow and learn.

One of your beliefs is that everyone else is more perfect than you. I'm not here to reassure you that's not true—that you're just as good as everyone else. Everyone is unique. It matters not what anyone else's path is or how they're doing on their path. All that matters is you. To focus on others and compare yourself to them is wasted energy, which takes you away from yourself and your soul path.

There will always be others further along than you. There will always be others at an earlier stage. What difference does it make? Does it keep you from loving and from doing the soul work you came here to do?

Tom: No.

Yeshua: Then why does it matter?

Tom: I guess it really doesn't matter.

Yeshua: It only matters if you believe that the perfect get loved, and the imperfect don't. The perfect get rewarded by God, and the imperfect don't. That belief is propagated by the Church. Would you say that's accurate?

Tom: Yes, although the Church does say that God's love is unconditional.

Yeshua: It says both, doesn't it?

Tom: Yes, yes.

Yeshua: "You must be good or perfect to get into heaven. You're a sinner, and you must always go beyond your sins." These are not my teachings or my beliefs. These ideas have hurt many people, and it sounds like you're among them.

Tom: Yes. I'm not worthy. That's what I've heard so often.

Yeshua: Here's my teaching. There are two aspects to your nature and your human divinity. There's the Masculine aspect, which is always already perfect—it's God in transcendent form. And there's the Feminine, which is God in immanent, human form, in manifestation, *which will never be perfect.* [Yeshua laughs heartily.] Certainly not according to your concepts of perfection. [Tom laughs.] And that's perfect for your soul growth and the lessons you came here to receive. Both aspects are true. They're true of you as an individual and of every aspect of your reality.

You could see these two aspects as two sides of the same coin: perfection and manifestation (which, in third-dimensional reality, is anything but perfect). Neither excludes the other. If you only see perfection, you're living in a dream. If you only see the lack of perfection, you're living separate from God. The ultimate union of the Masculine and Feminine is to see that you are both, your world is both, everything consists of both. And there's no conflict between the two. You might call it a paradox. These seeming opposites are simultaneously the case always.

Tom: I guess I stay more with the imperfection than the perfection.

Yeshua: Yes. Ironically, you do that because you love God so much and want to unite with God. So, you beat yourself up for your perceived shortcomings that keep you from God.

Tom: Yes, yes.

Yeshua: You must realize that's your pattern and indoctrination. And you must counter that. But you'll never counter it through your mind, Tom. It happens through your feelings. And you can't *think* about the feelings. You can't *think* about the divine qualities. These must be a *felt* activity.

Building the Muscle of Feeling

Yeshua: Can you contact your feelings right now?

Tom: Right now I have energies all over my body.

Yeshua: Yes! Can you focus on *feeling* that?

Tom: Is it a feeling of fear?

Yeshua: That's your mind trying to label and control it. Instead, notice what your mind is doing, and return to feeling. You're building a muscle. That muscle is never going to be built by sitting at home thinking about how to do the exercise. [Yeshua and Tom laugh.] You have to do the exercise!

Let's exercise in this moment. Exercise feeling without needing to know what the feeling is. The feeling may be clear to you, and that's fine. If it's not, don't try to figure it out with your mind because that will take you away from feeling. Simply follow the feeling.

[Silence as Tom engages the process]

Tom: The feeling is getting stronger and stronger.

Yeshua: Yes. Is it pleasurable/enjoyable or painful/disturbing?

Tom: Neither pleasurable nor disturbing. There's anxiety that I'm going to burst.

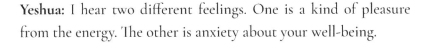

Yeshua: I hear two different feelings. One is a kind of pleasure from the energy. The other is anxiety about your well-being.

Tom: Yes.

Yeshua: Is there anything the feelings want to communicate? You can ask them.

Tom: A feeling is surfacing inside of wanting to weep.

Yeshua: Yes. Weeping is one of your signs. When you connect with your heart, tears tend to come.

Tom: Yes.

Yeshua: Don't hold yourself to the idea that tears will always accompany heart connection, even though that seems to be the pattern right now. At another stage, there may not be tears, and that's fine too.

Tears can be of joy or a release of past suppression. As you suppress less, there may be fewer tears. If they're tears of joy, the tears may continue. Either way, don't hold onto the experience because experience changes, but look to experience to show you what's happening.

Tom: As you were speaking, some energies arose toward my throat. Now I have two different feelings. One is a desire to weep, and the other is a feeling of wanting to throw up.

Yeshua: Yes. The feeling of wanting to throw up can be a cleansing or purification of past suppression.

Tom: It's like needing to go to the bathroom to get rid of what's inside.

Yeshua: Yes. Let yourself relax and open to it. That's the muscle we're engaging.

[Tom coughs.]

Yeshua: Coughing can be another way of cleansing, clearing.

[Silence]

I'm sensing peace. Is that what you're experiencing?

Tom: There's peace, but there's also disturbance. In coughing, I disturbed my lungs and thought, *With this coronavirus, I have to be careful because my lungs are delicate.*

Yeshua: You felt anxiety about your health.

Tom: Yes.

Yeshua: Because you want to protect your well-being.

Tom: Yes.

Yeshua: Let yourself drop into that longing to protect your well-being. Find the place in you that experiences that protection. Can you feel that?

Tom: What I feel is pain in my chest.

Yeshua: That's your physical symptom. Can you feel the place that knows the fullness of having your well-being protected?

Tom: I'm having difficulty getting out of my head. It's throbbing.

Yeshua: Is it painful?

Tom: Overloaded. I want to get down into my heart and set my mind aside.

Yeshua: But you're struggling to do that.

Tom: Yes, yes.

Yeshua: And your head is throbbing.

Tom: Yes.

Yeshua: I imagine there's an emotion connected with that—fear. You're afraid of going into your heart. Is that accurate?

Tom: The fear. *Am I going to find that place of protection of my well-being in my heart?* That's my head speaking again.

Yeshua: Yes. I'm hearing you want confidence that you're capable of this. Is that true?

Tom: That's right. We've gone through that confidence before.

Yeshua: It doesn't matter how many times we've gone through it. Your head wants to do it once and then either never do it again or hold onto it for dear life. [Yeshua and Tom laugh.] Neither is what we're trying to do. I'm going to ask your head to relax.

Tom: I almost want to take my head off and set it aside.

Yeshua: No need. I'm going to talk to your head. Head, are you needing trust that Tom can do what I'm asking?

Tom: Yes.

Yeshua: Head, what do you think is going to happen if Tom tries to do this?

Tom: He may not get there. Or if he does, he may find no well-being.

Yeshua: What would happen if that were the case?

Tom: My mind says, *I told you so.* I'm remembering a person I know who was afraid to go into her dreams for fear she'd fall to the bottom and hurt herself. Somebody suggested she stay with the dream and fall. The next night she did that, and when she got to the ground she bounced. All was well. [Tom starts weeping.] My heart hopes all will be well if I let go.

Yeshua: Yes. You want safety.

Tom: Yes.

Yeshua: Head, you're trying to protect Tom and keep him safe, aren't you?

Tom: Yes.

Yeshua: Thank you, head, for all your care and for wanting Tom to be safe.

Become You and Let God Work Through You

Tom: [weeping] I'm sorry.

Yeshua: What are you sorry about?

Tom: That I keep putting up obstacles to my path.

Yeshua: Your greatest obstacle is trying to be other than what you are.

Tom: I want to be like you, all put together.

Yeshua: You don't know what it is to be me.

Tom: I know. But I keep trying.

Yeshua: Yes. That is your great obstacle. Your work is not to become me but to become you. [Yeshua and Tom laugh.] To let God work through you.

Tom: [laughs] I guess if I was you, you wouldn't be necessary.

Yeshua: We have no idea what would be the case. Are you willing to become you?

Tom: Yes, I want to become me, even though I fear being me.

Yeshua: That fear has kept you from being you. *I* want you to become you. We all need you, and we all love you. You. Not someone else who's better than you. You.

Tom: Thank you. That's hard. [weeps]

Yeshua: It's very hard. You should have received this understanding as a young child from your mother and father, but they probably didn't know about it. Or perhaps it was your karma not to receive it but to come to this understanding as part of your life lesson. Whatever the reason, it's important. You came here to be you, not anyone else. You are absolutely loved in all ways as you.

Tom: No matter what I've done, how I've been . . .

Yeshua: Yes. This is not to say that you never need to grow, learn, or change. Those processes are included in being you. But they must rest on the foundation of an absolute knowing: You're loved as you are.

Tom: Thank you, thank you.

Yeshua: Yes. Have you ever loved in that way? Not because something or someone is perfect or you demand perfection. You love them through their wonderful and their difficult aspects, simply because you love them.

Tom: I love Ann that way.

Yeshua: Yes.

Tom: Even though some things irk me, I love her anyhow.

Yeshua: Right.

Tom: She's so wonderful to me. That's why I keep asking, how can she?

Yeshua: That's your old unlovable strategy coming through.

Tom: Yes.

Mourning Is Essential

Yeshua: You must be very real about the pain you've experienced from feeling that you're not lovable or good enough to be loved. There's mourning to do around that, which is feeling work. It's not something to think about or to try to figure out through its origins or history or anything like that. Do you understand what I'm saying?

Tom: Maybe just continue a little more.

Yeshua: A big impediment to building a feeling muscle is the programming that says you shouldn't mourn or grieve or be sad—that if you do, you're weak or a failure. That belief is totally wrong. The Feminine within you is starving for mourning. In many cultures there are no models for how to mourn. Instead, you receive these messages: *Mourning is negative, a waste of time. You'll get stuck in it—it's a sinkhole that will take you lower and lower, and you'll never get out. Beware! Stay away!* All that is false. Mourning is your next step in growing your feeling muscle, which you need in order to proceed.

Tom: What am I mourning? Not being perfect?

Yeshua: You're mourning the belief that you needed to be perfect or that you were never good enough. You're mourning that having that belief has hurt you so much. Can you relate to that?

Tom: Yes, yes, yes.

Yeshua: Mourning won't necessarily be quick or continuous. You may connect with your mourning for a while and then not connect with it. During the time of not connecting, the work continues, perhaps at a deeper level that you're not aware of. You may need a break for your own balance and well-being.

Trust the process, with its wisdom and intelligence. The more you think about it the more you'll block it. If you notice yourself trying to analyze or understand what's happening, let go. Return to feeling and prayer. Ask for healing of this pattern in whatever way is best.

Tom: What you say feels right.

Yeshua: I'm glad. May I change to a different topic?

Tom: Yes, yes.

Love Is More Than a Feeling

Yeshua: I want to respond to what you said about not feeling love for Ann.

From my point of view, love is much deeper than a feeling. Feelings come and go. They change all the time, like the weather. You can't look to the weather to say whether the sun exists. Sometimes it's sunny, sometimes it's cloudy, and sometimes it's rainy. Weather comes and goes, but the sun is always there.

That's the nature of love. It's the nature of all your inner divine qualities. They're always there. If you become attached to certain feelings, you'll be tormented. With love, sometimes we have open-hearted feelings, warm feelings, even ecstatic feelings, joyful feelings. But if you identify love as only those feelings, you're in trouble. Love can also be excruciating, maddening, and frustrating [laughs]. I'm sure you've experienced this as well. Love can be heartbreaking. Love can manifest many different feelings. Don't measure love by feelings. Feelings exist simply to point you to love.

If love is strong and steady, often the feeling is more a sense of peace. There will be times of pleasurable weather—beautiful, sunny days—and times of weather that you don't enjoy. But the love continues. Do you understand?

Tom: Yes. Thank you for that.

Yeshua: It's very important. The mind can be so misguided. Don't go by your mind. The mind wants to hold on. *If I have this feeling, then I know I'm in love.* No. Love is much deeper.

Tom: Thank you.

Yeshua: You're welcome.
Feelings coming and going are part of the nature of the Feminine. The Feminine is always in flux and change. The inner divinity is the Masculine, which never changes. It is eternal and infinite.

Both are true. Don't look to just the Feminine to see if you're in love, or you'll be in great trouble. [Yeshua and Tom laugh.] Let your feelings guide you to your inner divine qualities—which is your eternal, infinite Masculine. Then your Feminine and Masculine can join in holy matrimony. Does that make sense?

Tom: Yes, it does.

Yeshua: Wonderful. I have a sense we are complete for today.

Tom: Yes, yes. Thank you so much, Yeshua.

Yeshua: You're very welcome. I love you tremendously.

Tom: Thank you so much. I love you too.

Yeshua: Many blessings, my dear one.

Tom: Thank you. Till we meet again.

Yeshua: Indeed.

Tom: Say hi to Mary Magdalene.

Yeshua: [chuckles] Always.

SIXTEEN

Breathing Fresh Air

*Y*eshua: Hello, beloved, this is Yeshua. I am here with my beloved Mary Magdalene. We're both so happy to join you again for our ongoing dialogue, which has been so fruitful, so valuable. I thank you for participating with us throughout this time and for making this work available to all who will receive it in the future.

Let us begin for today. What would you like to share, Tom?

Tom: Thank you, Yeshua and Mary Magdalene, for coming back and for our last conversation. You listened to my stories so lovingly and emphatically said you loved *me* over and over again. It touched my heart so deeply.

The last few days I've had contrasting experiences. I asked for dreams to show me how I might speak about this with you, Yeshua. I had two dreams that showed me what happens when the Feminine and my feeling nature are excluded from my life. I feel limited, less than, not enough, embarrassed, lost. When I'm with the Feminine and my feelings, there's a brightness, joy, celebration, and an aliveness.

I realized our last conversation could have been our final one; it was so beautiful for me. I felt especially moved when you so tenderly said, "I love *you*." I think you were pointing your finger at me as if to say, "It's you I love. Not somebody you'd like to be or somebody you could be. You."

Still, I felt anxious, which I shared with Mercedes. She replied by email this morning: "Tom, I think you're overthinking everything. Go back to when you realized Yeshua loved you. Stay with that." She's a wise woman.

After breakfast the sun blazed with warmth and light everywhere. The pictures, walls, colors—everything looked so beautiful. I simply gazed at it all and then closed my eyes.

Instead of being on the exterior of my body, as I've typically experienced the last few days, my feelings were inside my chest: a feeling of goodness. As I sat there with that feeling, I recalled a passage from *The Diary of Anne Frank*: "Today the sun is shining. The sky is a deep blue. There is a lovely breeze and I'm longing, so longing for everything. . . I feel my heart beating as if it's saying, 'Can't you satisfy my longing at last?'"

I, too, have often thought that in my life: *Can't you satisfy my longing at last?* Today I'm so grateful for these feelings of goodness and aliveness, well-being and harmony. I appreciate my dreams mirroring who I am, showing me the way to go. I feel so whole and grateful.

Yeshua: This is wonderful news! Congratulations! It's the most excellent report you could offer. [Yeshua and Tom laugh.] Truly you have received exactly what you needed. It's also true that we could have stopped with the last session. For indeed, that is where you received it. But it's wonderful to meet again and confirm all this.

Your understanding that came through your dreams is an interesting mirroring. You said you feel limited or "not enough" when you're cut off from the Feminine. And when you include the Feminine and are connected to her—tell me your words again?

Tom: I feel a brightness, an aliveness, like breathing fresh air.

Yeshua: Yes, yes. This is a mirroring of your earlier life as a priest, when you were cut off from the Feminine. You chose to leave that to be connected to the Feminine, specifically in the form of your wife. You chose to live with the Feminine and love the Feminine through your wife. I am so happy for you.

Tom: Thank you. I'm happy too.

Oscillation

Yeshua: It's worth acknowledging that there will likely be times when you don't feel as connected to this, times of going back and forth, as you did after our last session. When letting go of an old pattern and assuming a new one, a period of oscillation is natural as you go back and forth between the old and the new.

You now have this excellent clarity to help you during such oscillations. The old pattern is to live in your mind and exclude the Feminine. The new pattern is to connect through your feelings with the Feminine and unite your mind and your heart. We have done this a number of times, and you are now beginning to do this on your own.

You also have support, if you desire it. Mercedes is an excellent support for you through her courses and her individual work. Her books can also be a support. *Mary Magdalene Beckons* may make much more sense to you after these dialogues. You have a touchstone, a grounding with which to receive that teaching and understand it at a much deeper level. You can always call on us, for we are here for you. Mercedes can help you with that too.

Most importantly, you have opened to your own source of help, your own empowerment, through your feelings, your body, and your dreams. Dreams are an energetic manifestation, which is the Feminine. But you also receive insight, instruction, guidance, and wisdom, which is part of the Masculine. Through your dreams, you experience the fourth-dimensional aspects of the Feminine and the Masculine—which work in tandem, union, and harmony to support you—and that is excellent.

Tom: Thank you so much. The other day, I said to Ann, "I'm not finished yet. I was hoping to be complete." But you told me that if I were perfect, I would not need to be here. [Tom and Yeshua laugh.]

Yeshua: And that is so. You are opening to the next level of growth and exploration in your soul journey. So it is for all.

Tom: Yes. Ann and I agreed it would be good for us to take the Magdalene Heart Path course from Mercedes.

Yeshua: Yes. That will be even more supportive and strengthen this process for you even more. That would be an excellent avenue.

Tom: I wish we lived closer to Mercedes.

Yeshua: Indeed. But you have your technology, which has served you well.

Tom: Yes. Right now we're isolated because of the coronavirus.

Yeshua: This isolation can be another motivation for moving into the fourth dimension, where you will not be limited to such physical things.

Tom: Yes, yes.

Letting Go

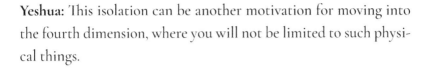

Yeshua: I want to mention one more thing. Because this is our last session, you may go through sadness at letting go of our connection as we have known it through this time, which has been sweet and wonderful. Mary Magdalene and I feel the same. It's bittersweet to let go because we have so enjoyed this.

If that is what you experience—or if it's not—do not make a problem out of it. Whatever you experience is perfect for you. You know your path through it now. Open to it, and let it guide you to whatever you need for healing, deepening, and moving toward your next steps.

Tom: I'm going to miss both of you.

Yeshua: Indeed. And we shall miss our time with you.

Tom: It's been such a privilege and honor to be invited to these dialogues. You and Mary Magdalene have responded to my questions with patience, love, and tenderness. I'm especially grateful to you for getting me out of my major questions and into my inner journey. I didn't expect that when we started. [Tom and Yeshua laugh.] You did, but I didn't.

Yeshua: I can't help myself. [Yeshua and Tom laugh.] My soul's mission is to support people in their spiritual growth, and it is all my soul wants to do.

Tom: So often I blocked you by going back to my questions, but you kept pulling me forward into my inner journey. I'm so grateful for that.

There's a story about a man and his small son. The gentleman took his son along to a meeting where his son started making a lot of noise. Not knowing what to do, the man found a magazine with a map of the world inside. He tore the map into pieces and gave them to the little boy. "Here, put this together," he said. In no time, the little boy gave it back to his father.

"How did you put it back together so quickly?" the father asked.

"I looked at the other side, which was a picture of a man," the boy said. "When I put the man together, the world fell into place." That's how it will be. When I put myself together, it'll help the world fall into place.

Yeshua: That's delightful and beautiful. Thank you so much. We love you so, so much.

Tom: I love you so much too. Thank you, thank you, thank you. And I love Ann and Mercedes. I really appreciate Mercedes. Please send her blessings and good wishes.

Yeshua: Absolutely. To clarify one last thing: even as we miss you, we are always with you and never separate.

Tom: Thank you.

Yeshua: We love you for eternity.

Tom: Thank you so very much. I love you too.

Yeshua: Blessings, blessings, blessings.

Notes

1. Mary Magdalene was a follower of Jesus in the Bible. Many believe she was Jesus's wife.

2. "Yeshua" is the Hebrew/Aramaic name for Jesus. Many believe Jesus was called Yeshua two thousand years ago in Israel. In Mercedes's channeled sessions, Mary Magdalene has always called Jesus "Yeshua." Accordingly, the name Yeshua is used throughout these sessions. In Chapter 9, Yeshua clarifies that our names for him are not important: "The names are always for you. You may call me whatever you choose."

3. See endnote 2.

4. See endnote 1.

5. The Eucharist is a Christian rite involving the sharing of bread and wine as part of the Mass. It's based upon biblical passages (Mark 14:22–24 and par.) in which Jesus is said to have given his disciples bread and wine, saying the bread was his body and the wine his blood.

6. John 6:53

7. The Essenes were a Jewish sect in Judea from the second century BCE to the first century CE. Many believe they practiced vegetarianism.

8. John 13:23

9. The Council of Nicaea was an assembly of Christian bishops convened by the Roman Emperor Constantine I in 325 CE to define Christian doctrine and structures.

10. Mark 16:11 and par.

11. John 21:15

12. In the book *Mary Magdalene Beckons*, Mary Magdalene presents a model of our universe that includes twelve dimensions. The fourth

dimension is the next plane of reality beyond the third dimension. This plane is energetically rather than physically based. The full model of the twelve dimensions, including the fourth dimension, is described in detail in *Mary Magdalene Beckons* by Mercedes Kirkel.

13. Luke 22:44

14. The Feminine and the Masculine are key concepts in the teaching of Yeshua and Mary Magdalene. The terms refer to the archetypal Feminine and Masculine that reside within all of us (regardless of our gender) and within all of manifestation. The twin concepts are similar to the concept of yin and yang in Eastern philosophy. Yeshua and Mary use the terms "Divine Feminine" or "Divine Masculine" when referring to the Feminine or Masculine aspects of God or our human divinity.

The Feminine aspects of our humanness relate to our body, energy, emotions, sexuality, and heart. The highest form of the Feminine is pure love. The Masculine aspects of our humanity relate to our mind and willpower. The highest form of the Masculine is pure consciousness.

Yeshua and Mary Magdalene teach that to transition into the fourth dimension, a being must become strong in all aspects of both the Feminine and the Masculine, which includes coming into balance, harmony, and union *between* the Feminine and the Masculine. An in-depth explanation of the Masculine and the Feminine can be found in *Mary Magdalene Beckons* by Mercedes Kirkel.

15. Ascension is the process of spiritual transformation that leads beings of the third dimension into progressively higher dimensions of reality. For a full discussion of the higher dimensions, see *Mary Magdalene Beckons* by Mercedes Kirkel.

16. The fourth dimension is primarily focused on two components of our being. The first is our etheric or energetic component. The second is the astral component, which includes our emotional and our mental aspects. There's also a physical component to the fourth dimension, but it's much lighter or more fluid than in the third dimension. One way that most people experience the fourth dimension is through their dreams.

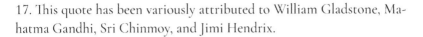

17. This quote has been variously attributed to William Gladstone, Mahatma Gandhi, Sri Chinmoy, and Jimi Hendrix.

18. John 4:10

19. The term "Magdalene Heart Path" refers to the teaching that Mary gave to Mercedes in *Mary Magdalene Beckons*.

20. John 4:16

21. The Magdalene Heart Path course is an online and video course based upon Mary Magdalene's teaching in *Mary Magdalene Beckons*. To learn more about the course, go to www.mercedeskirkel.com.

22. See endnote 19.

23. Yeshua is referring to the #MeToo movement, a social movement begun by women to publicize their personal experiences of abusive sexual behavior, including events occurring in institutions of power.

24. See endnote 23.

25. John 14:12

26. The term "inner divine quality" is Mary Magdalene's term for an aspect of our inner divinity that we're guided to through our feelings. For a fuller explanation of inner divine qualities and how they relate to feelings, see *Mary Magdalene Beckons* by Mercedes Kirkel.

27. John 14:15–17

About the Author

MERCEDES KIRKEL is a multi-award-winning, bestselling author and channel for Mary Magdalene and Yeshua.

In the summer of 2010, Mary Magdalene began coming to Mercedes daily, giving extraordinary messages for humanity's evolution and spiritual growth. That was the birth of the first two books of the Magdalene Teachings: *Mary Magdalene Beckons: Join the River of Love* and *Sublime Union: A Woman's Sexual Odyssey Guided by Mary Magdalene*. Mary Magdalene and Yeshua continue to communicate through Mercedes, delivering illuminating messages about the sacred partnership of the Divine Feminine and Masculine and guiding people in their spiritual evolution.

Based in New Mexico, Mercedes offers online courses and private sessions as well as in-person events. Her specialties include guidance from Mary Magdalene, Yeshua, and other beings of light; heart coaching; and spiritual support.

To learn more about Mercedes and her work, visit:
www.mercedeskirkel.com.

Other Books by Mercedes Kirkel

Mary Magdalene Beckons:
Join the River of Love
Book One of The Magdalene Teachings

In this multi-award-winning book, Mary Magdalene gives twenty-five extraordinary messages for opening the heart, uniting the Feminine and the Masculine, and growing spiritually.

"An incredible gift . . . A great deal of insight into . . . spiritual beliefs." —*Seattle Post-Intelligencer* Book Review

"Mary . . . is unmistakable through her words and the author's insights." —Lisa Marshall, Examiner.com

"An outstanding spiritual self-help book." —Readers' Favorite Book Review

"Highly recommended." —Midwest Book Review

Sublime Union: *A Woman's Sexual Odyssey Guided by Mary Magdalene*
Book Two of The Magdalene Teachings

In this #1 bestselling book, Mary Magdalene reveals the sexual practices of priestesses in the ancient Egyptian temple of Isis, interwoven with Mercedes's stirring story of applying the teachings with her partner.

"I highly recommend this thrilling read." —Christiane Northrup, MD, NY Times bestselling author

"A multifaceted jewel of a book that shimmers with light and love." —Diana Richardson, author of *The Heart of Tantric Sex* and *Slow Sex*

"A must read for all those on the Magdalene path." —Anaiya Sophia, author of *Sacred Sexual Union*

Learn more about Mercedes's books
and other offerings at: www.mercedeskirkel.com